"In *Perfect Pan Pizza*—as detailed as it is enjoyable to read—the master bread baker dives into the unexplored depths of pan pizzas. Reinhart explains complex baking concepts with such ease that his pages are useful to the novice and the professional alike. I feel as if he's sitting next to me reading aloud, helping me make the best pizza I've ever eaten."

—SCOTT WIENER, owner of Scott's Pizza Tours

"No pizza pan is as deep as baking guru Peter Reinhart's knowledge of four-cornered styles like Detroit, Roman, and Sicilian. In *Perfect Pan Pizza*, Reinhart is in *your* corner, acting as your teacher and personal pizza coach, helping you build the skills of an accomplished home pizzaiolo."

—DANIEL YOUNG, author of *Where to Eat Pizza*

"Peter Reinhart is the Buddha of Bread. He is one with dough, and that makes him the Pundit of Pizza, too. With Reinhart's masterful dough recipes, you'll be baking up all kinds of crunchy, cheesy pan pizzas in no time. Follow the Buddha into these pages, watch his practiced hands, and you'll soon be pulling incredible Sicilian, Roman, and Detroit-style square pies from your oven."

—DAVID JOACHIM, coauthor of *Mastering Pizza*

Date: 7/3/19

641.8248 REI
Reinhart, Peter,
Perfect pan pizza : square pies to make at home, from Roman,

PERFECT PAN PIZZA

PERFECT PAN PIZZA

Square Pies to Make at Home,
from Roman, Sicilian, and Detroit,
to Grandma Pies and Focaccia

PETER REINHART
Photographs by Johnny Autry

TEN SPEED PRESS
California | New York

1	**Introduction**	55	Spicy Oil
5	**Getting Started: Tips and Tricks**	56	Caramelized Balsamic Onion Marmalade
5	Tools and Equipment	58	Caramelized Garlic Cloves and Garlic Oil
6	Pans	59	Secret Sauces
8	Ingredients		
11	Portioning and Panning the Dough	63	**CH 3 | DEEP-PAN DETROIT-STYLE PIZZA**
		69	The Classic Red Stripe
17	**CH 1 | IT'S ALL ABOUT THE CRUST**	73	Bacon and Egg
27	White Flour Dough	75	Pepperoni Deluxe
29	Whole Grain Country-Style Dough	78	Kundalini Cauliflower
33	Naturally Leavened Dough	81	Philly-Style Roast Pork with Broccoli Rabe
		85	Mushrooms to the Max
43	**CH 2 | SAUCES AND SPECIALTY TOPPINGS**	88	Beef Brisket with Burnt Ends
		91	Banh Mi
46	Crushed Tomato Pizza Sauce	95	Veggie "Pepperoni"
49	All-Purpose Marinara Pizza Sauce	97	Olive and Artichoke Medley
51	Pesto Genovese	100	Lemon, Broccoli, and Garlic
54	Herb Oil		

CONTENTS

102 The SCLT (Smoked Chicken, Lettuce, and Tomatoes)

105 Reuben

109 Spaghetti and Meatballs

112 Philly Cheesesteak

115 Motor City Hawaiian

117 Garlic Lovers' Italian Sausage

121 CH 4 | FOCACCIA, SCHIACCIATA, SICILIAN-STYLE, AND ROMAN-STYLE PIZZAS

125 Focaccia Bianca with Herb Oil

127 Blue Cheese, Balsamic Onion Marmalade, and Walnut Focaccia

130 Herbed Tomato and Pesto Focaccia

132 Bacon and Potato Focaccia

134 Fruited Focaccia with Citrus Glaze

137 Grape and Anise Schiacciata

142 Classic Pepperoni

143 Umberto's-Style Grandma Pie

146 Spicy Amatriciana

149 Lemon, Spinach, and Cheese Curd

151 White Clams Casino

153 Puttanesca

155 "Greek"

159 The Classics: Rossa (Red) and Bianca (White)

161 Grape Tomato and Ricotta Cream

165 Susan's Rosemary-Garlic Potatoes

167 Nduja Cioppino

170 Sweet Onion-Bechamel with Mortadella

173 Avocado "Scampi"

175 Resources

178 Glossary

181 Acknowledgments

182 Index

INTRODUCTION

WHY THIS BOOK AND WHY NOW?

This book is a celebration of pizzas made in pans, perennial classics that are now being reinvented by those who know how to evoke their full flavor potential. Pizza, I would risk saying, is the most popular food in the world. There are many forms and variations of pizza, but in the end pizza is simply dough with something on it. And yet, in its simplicity, it is amazingly delicious. Something magical happens when dough is combined with a topping; making pizza the perfect flavor-delivery system. Dough with something on it just works.

In the United States and in a number of other countries, many pizza permutations have come and gone. There are, however, some styles that have earned perennial popularity, like the Neapolitan-inspired round pizza with sauce and cheese, which has come to be regarded, by many (but not all), as the prototype on which all other pizzas are based. Other configurations with different names have, from time to time, attempted to capture some of that dough-with-something-on-it caché, such as focaccia, *schiacciata*, flatbreads, quesadillas, tostadas, and even grilled cheese sandwiches (albeit, a sandwich is more of a dough with something in it). All of these are spokes of the same wheel, all of them simply variations on a theme but one dominated by the word *pizza*. For example, some of the best-tasting pizzas at this moment are actually, in the strictest sense of the word, focaccia, but are marketed as pizza because the public (outside of Genoa) loves and trusts the term *pizza* more than it does *focaccia*.

Some of the types of pizza that fall within this pan-pizza subcategory include focaccia (the pizza of Northern Italy, most notably associated with Genoa in Liguria), *schiacciata* (the Tuscan version of focaccia), Sicilian-style (perhaps inspired by, though different from, the original *sfingiuni* of Sicily but now a designated style of its own), and the two currently hottest subcategories of them all, Roman-style *al taglio* ("baked in a pan") and Detroit-style deep-pan pizza, revered for its crispy, cheesy frico edge (more on this later) and its crackly, buttery undercrust. Detroit-style deep-pan pizza is not a new idea or style, having been "invented" almost eighty years ago by former autoworker Gus Guerra. Now you can find it under other names in many cities other than Detroit. What is surprising is that it has taken so long for it to become so popular. We'll get into the specifics in chapter 4.

Until recently, few knew about Detroit's unique square pizza, and even those who were from Detroit didn't call it Detroit-style. Then, after sixty years of regional obscurity and cultish secrecy, this newly named Detroit-style, long in Chicago's shadow, finally became an idea whose time had come, and now to our great benefit it's popping up everywhere.

We have arrived at a unique, paradigm-changing moment in which artisan pizza masters are turning out the best versions of these styles that have ever been produced. As a result, the hidden gems, not just the sexy wood-fired and coal-fired classics but the more homey pan-style versions— the deep square-pan and sheet-pan styles (the focaccia, Sicilian, and Grandma pies) and now even the newly emerging Roman-style *al taglio* cut-with-a-scissors pizzas—are transcending their old neighborhood standbys and are being given newer expression. Today's artisans are pushing the envelope and redefining the realm of the possible in this paradoxically simple-yet-complex perfect flavor-delivery system called pizza.

Culinary artisanship is meeting global archetype, and we, the public, are the beneficiaries of a new golden age of pizza expression. The purpose of this book is to show you, the home cook, how to replicate the artisan techniques that have brought about this pan-pizza renaissance and thereby create pizzas equal to anything you will find at a pan-style pizzeria. This is not a tribute book about the many landmark pan-pizza establishments doing great work, though many of them, like Buddy's in Detroit, Brown Dog in Telluride, Liguria Bakery in San Francisco, Pizzarium in Rome and Chicago, Triple Beam in Los Angeles, and many others, have provided inspiration. It is a book about how you can make your own pan pizzas with the same explosive flavor perfection as the pies from those iconic places. To help you achieve that goal, I have included techniques that I've discovered or developed during my thirty years as an artisan baker, pizza maker, and educator. Happily, I've been able to combine them all in an easy method so that whether you are an experienced or a novice cook, you will soon be making not just good but truly memorable pizzas for your friends and family.

As I discuss the different styles, I'll explain more about the methodology and supplemental ingredients and provide recipes not only for the dough but also for the toppings. I've met many pizza masters through my research and my ongoing website PizzaQuest.com, and based on the information they have shared with me, I have been able to distill the essential secrets of their successes and methods. The pizza world is a generous community, so there are very few secrets. This is because the truly great *pizzaioli* know that the real secret is in the craft itself, which is acquired only through relentless practice. As the great American pizza master Chris Bianco told me, "I can teach people my techniques, but I can't teach them to care as much as I care." This observation is probably the most important takeaway from all my research and inquiry into what separates good from great: it boils down to how much you care.

As you achieve success through these very accessible formulas and pan-pizza recipes, I hope you will be inspired to care as much as those artisans who bring honor to their craft. Even if you never become a professional pizza maker (only a very few will ever choose to work that hard), I believe that by tapping into a level of greatness through these pan pizzas, you will experience the sought-after, memorable sound of crust and all that comes with it. When you experience greatness in anything, even pizza, it spills over into the rest of your life and changes you forever.

In the following chapters, you will find recipes for sauces, condiments, and over thirty variations of pan pizzas. Although this is not an exhaustive list of recipes, it will provide a foundation and inspiration from which you can create an infinite number of variations of your own. These recipes also include commentaries and options for ingredient substitutions and tweaks. There is also a Resources section (page 175) with suggestions for finding ingredients, tools, books, and more information.

Yes, I'm promising you a lot here, so let's get started!

GETTING STARTED: TIPS AND TRICKS

Before we dig into the recipes, I want to give you a basic list of the tools and ingredients you will need, including information on the various styles of pans you can use for the pizzas in this book (see page 6) and the cheeses that I think work best (see page 9), as well as a primer on the basic method for portioning and panning the pizza dough (see page 11). Take the time to read this section before you begin.

TOOLS AND EQUIPMENT

You don't need many tools to make these pizzas. Even a stand mixer is not mandatory. However, if you do have one, such as a Kitchen Aid or other brand of planetary mixer (so called because the hook or paddle moves around the bowl like planets around the sun), it will make mixing easier. You can also mix the dough in a mixing bowl with a large mixing spoon or with your hands.

I do, however, have one caveat: although you can make pizza using volume measuring tools, the use of a scale is more likely to give you the best results. In case you don't have a scale, I've provided volume equivalents, but these are not guaranteed to be as precise as measurements by weight. The reason for this discrepancy is that everyone scoops flour or eyeballs their water measuring cups differently, sometimes packing the flour, sometimes aerating it, and so forth. That being the case, I've also given some tactile and visual prompts, such as how the dough should be supple and somewhat sticky rather

than firm and stiff. Even if you use a scale and weigh everything perfectly, different brands of flour can absorb water differently, but if you "listen" to your dough, it will "tell" you if it needs more water or perhaps more flour. As you develop a feel for working with this soft, sticky dough, it will become easier to use, so resist the temptation of adding more flour that the dough might not need. The more troublesome problem is when the dough is too stiff because the flour may have been packed too tightly or the brand is very dry and absorbs more water. It's easier to add more flour to an overly sticky dough than to add more water to an overly stiff dough, but you can do it by kneading in additional water, a teaspoon at a time, until the dough feels appropriately supple. The bottom line: If you don't have a kitchen scale, use the measuring tools you have and listen to your dough as you mix it to find out if it needs adjusting.

Aside from a scale, the two most essential tools for dough makers are plastic bowl scrapers and metal dough blades, also known as pastry blades, bench blades, or benchers. Both of these are widely available at kitchenware stores. You will also need the following:

- Sharp knives, both chef-style and serrated
- Pallet knife with a rounded end (also known as an icing spatula), or a metal burger flipper, for removing a baked pizza without damaging the pan
- Mixing bowls of various sizes
- Plastic wrap

- Spray oil (I suggest olive oil sprays, which are now widely available.)
- Cutting boards, both large and small
- Roller-style pizza knife (not required but very useful)
- Parchment paper or silicone mats (aka Silpats)
- Pots and pans of various sizes
- Standard home oven-size (12 by 17 by 1-inch) sheet pans

PANS

There are many shapes and sizes of pans that will work for these recipes, but the amount of dough you use will vary according to the type of pizza or focaccia you are making, and the size of the pan, so consult the chart on page 15 for dough weights for pans of various sizes.

Many of us already possess sheet or cake pans that will work for the deep-pan style, and in the Resources section (page 175) you will find links to companies that produce pans for professionals designed specifically for deep-pan pizza. I have also had success buying less expensive (and thus, less durable but still adequate) pans at stores that sell kitchen supplies, such as Bed Bath & Beyond, Target, and Sur la Table. I suggest square or rectangular baking pans of nearly any size, with a depth of either 2 or 3 inches. If you don't have a square or rectangular pan, you can use a round 8, 9, or 10 inch-diameter cake pan (while square or rectangular pans are more customary for baking Detroit-style deep-pan pizzas, there is no rule against round versions).

For the deep-pan pizzas, I do not recommend standard home oven-size sheet pans (called half-sheet pans by professional bakers, who use full-size [17 by 24-inch] sheet pans in their large commercial ovens). These pans typically come with 1-inch sides, which are too shallow for a true deep-pan style, because the cheese will bubble over the side and into the oven. These pans are precisely what you need, however, for focaccia, *schiacciata*, Sicilian-style, and Roman-style pizzas.

Another consideration is material. While glass (Pyrex) baking pans do work for deep-pan pizzas, I suggest using metal pans, whether steel or cast aluminum. There is no question that steel pans, such as the ones typically used for the original Detroit-style pizzas, do a great job of conducting heat and baking excellent pizzas. However, based on my conversations with manufacturers who produce many varieties for home cooks as well as for professionals (see Resources, page 175), and what I have discovered in my own test baking, I have found that almost any baking pan, whether it be a steel, glass, or cast-aluminum sheet or cake pan, will do a great job providing proper heat distribution for a crisp, golden undercrust. So, if you want to replicate the original Detroit-style versions, you might consider purchasing some of the fabricated steel pans with folded, welded sides and corners. However, be assured that the nonwelded, smooth-cornered pans work just as well as the blue steel–welded pans.

INGREDIENTS

While most pizza fanatics obsess about crust, the quality of the toppings is also essential, much like the icing on a cake. It is important to remember that when you are applying

ingredients for toppings such as canned tomato products, olive oil, or fresh meats and produce, the rule of thumb is more is not always better; better quality is better. Therefore, seek out the highest-quality ingredients that you can find or afford and use them judiciously.

Measuring

While the Master Dough formulas make exactly enough dough (about 38 oz./1.02 kg) for one 11 by 17-inch sheet pan of focaccia, you will have to cut and weigh pieces of dough when using smaller pans, such as the square and rectangular pans for deep-pan pizza, round cake pans, or the pans for Roman-style and Sicilian-style pizzas. The suggested amount for these various pans and types of pizza are found in the chart on page 15.

The ingredients listed for toppings also will vary in amount depending on the style of pizza you are making. The toppings for focaccia are designed for one pan, but the toppings for the smaller pans are based on the yield listed with each recipe, usually enough for two medium-size pans. You will need to increase or decrease the amount depending on the number and size of the pizzas you plan to make. If you made more topping than you need, the extra will keep well in the refrigerator or freezer and can be used at a later time or served as a side dish.

Flour

To achieve the stellar crust that makes these pizzas really special, the ideal flour for the dough in this book is unbleached bread flour or high-protein whole wheat or sprouted whole wheat flour. All-purpose flour and Italian double

zero (aka tipo 00) can work, and some pizza makers do use them, but I've found that bread flour, any commercial brand, especially if it's unbleached, is ideal for flavor, texture, and structure, and I have formulated the recipes with this flour in mind. My preference for unbleached bread flour is also based on what I consider to be an important feature that bleached flour just doesn't deliver: aroma. The bleaching process makes flour whiter and thus more desirable for some cakes and pastries, and it may even strengthen flour and help it to bond better with fats like butter. In other words, bleached flour may, arguably, make better biscuits. However, using unbleached flour with bread and pizza creates a lovely, almost seductive aroma, which is a great part of the joy of home baking.

That said, if you happen to have bleached flour and want to use it, you can still make great pizza dough using these formulas. Those who choose to work with unbleached bread flour will find it at most markets, and any reliable brand such as General Mills, King Arthur, Bob's Red Mill, Central Milling, or Pillsbury will work. Or, if you have a local mill that you support or if you grind your own flour (kudos to you!), you can make these formulas work by adjusting the amount of water as needed.

Leavening

These doughs can all be successfully made with commercial yeast, but I have also provided a formula for naturally fermented dough, also known as sourdough (page 36). Though these dough recipes were developed using instant yeast (aka IDY or instant dry yeast), you can

WISCONSIN BRICK CHEESE

A Wisconsin made washed rind cow's milk cheese with excellent melting properties. It was originally developed by Swiss born cheese maker John Jossi in 1877 while working in a Limburger cheese factory in New York. He created Brick to be a less "smelly" cheese by using lower amounts of bacterial rub during the aging process. He then brought the process to Wisconsin, where he taught his method to many other cheese makers. There are a now a number of Wisconsin cheese companies that produce this cheese, among them Zimmerman Cheese, Widmer's (probably the closest in method to the original Jossi version), and Klondike Cheese, as well as many others. Paul Witke, of Zimmerman Cheese,

suggested to me that a more available and affordable cheese, with similar buttery flavor properties is Muenster. Brick cheese has a close association with Detroit-style deep-pan pizzas. It also has a wonderful buttery texture and flavor and it melts beautifully. However, it is not easy to find at retail markets, and there are many other cheeses that make good substitutions. The cheese that performs most like brick cheese in terms of buttery flavor and creaminess is Muenster, but combining mozzarella and Cheddar, or fontina and provolone, are also excellent swap-outs. In some of the following recipes, specific alternatives are suggested.

substitute fresh or active dry yeast. There are a couple of reasons why I developed my formulas using instant yeast. The first is that it is much easier to use than active dry yeast (ADY). It is called instant yeast not because it makes the dough rise instantly or faster but because it dissolves instantly when it gets hydrated during mixing. So, you can add it directly into the dry ingredients without having to bloom it first in warm water. Both forms of dry yeast (IDY and ADY) can be kept for months (even years) in airtight containers in either the refrigerator or freezer. (I keep mine in the freezer.)

Cheese

Cheese is a matter of personal preference, and many of us have our favorite types and brands. There are countless types of cheese that will work with these pizzas, far too many to list, but there are certain cheeses that are guaranteed to deliver great flavor and creamy, oozy texture. Among them are the following cheeses, which are cited in one or more recipes in this book. If you are a cheese connoisseur and want to swap a cheese listed in the recipe for one of your favorites, feel free to do so. Obviously, creamy melting cheeses with a flavor profile that matches well with the other toppings is a must, but if you are a cheese lover, you already know that.

You will notice that in many of the deep-pan recipes, I recommend cutting the cheese into small cubes. Cubed cheese takes a bit longer to melt and caramelize than shredded or grated cheese, and since the thicker deep-pan pizzas take longer to bake than Neapolitan-style pizzas do, the delayed melting of the cubed cheese allows time for the dough to properly bake, caramelize, and crisp without the cheese getting burned in the process.

Here are cheeses most likely to be available and appropriate for most of the pizzas in this book:

- Brick
- Cheddar
- Chèvre or fresh goat cheese
- Crescenza
- Feta
- Fontina
- Gruyère and other Swiss cheeses
- Jack
- Kasseri
- Mascarpone
- Meunster
- Mozzarella (low-moisture "pizza cheese" as well as fresh mozzarella)
- Parmesan, Romano, Asiago, and dry provolone
- Ricotta
- Smoked cheeses (like mozzarella, Gouda, and Cheddar)
- Taleggio

PORTIONING AND PANNING THE DOUGH

You can use virtually any shape or size pan to make the pizzas in this book. After making the dough, you'll simply need to weigh out the appropriate portion for the pan you're using (see page 15). You can do this either by putting the portioned dough into the pan before the final rise in the fridge or on the following day, after the bulk dough has gone through this final rest and has fully risen in the refrigerator (a cold fermentation technique known as retarding the dough). Both are valid options.

The advantage of portioning the dough before the overnight retarding is that it saves a step the following day, when you begin "dimpling," or pressing out the dough with your finger tips to fill the pan; it also saves about an hour of rising time. The disadvantage is that the pan may take up too much space in your refrigerator, in which case the bowl or container method is better. On the other hand, the disadvantage of the dough in bulk is that when you divide and weigh it for panning, the gluten tightens up, making it more difficult to spread the dough in the pan, adding about an hour of additional resting time to the process (which has been factored into the recipe instructions). Yet this method does save refrigerator space and allows you to retard more dough than you need for one pizza. The dough also will hold very nicely in the refrigerator for 3 or 4 days for subsequent bakes, or can be frozen for up to 3 months.

Dimpling

There are many ways to fill a pan with dough. In theory, you could use a rolling pin to stretch the dough and then lay it in the pan, or you could stretch it as you would round Neapolitan dough. But the doughs in this book use a high-hydration method, which results in a sticky pizza dough that is also very elastic as a result of stretching and folding (see the following section) and requires resting periods during the panning stage to prevent the dough from shrinking back to its original size. The rest periods allow the gluten to relax, and the dimpling method (see below) allows the dough to stretch without being forced or overworked. While it may require more time than aggressively forcing the dough to fill the pan, dough that is handled in this manner will produce desirable large and irregular holes in the baked crust, with a tender interior and a creamy mouthfeel.

How Much Dough and Cheese Do I Need?

With the Sicilian-style, Grandma, Roman-style, and focaccia recipes in this book, the amount of dough and cheese weights for each style is provided, based on baking in a standard 12 by 17 by 1-inch sheet pan. (In most instances the recipes call for the full weight of the dough recipe itself.) But for the Detroit-style deep-pan pizzas, which require a taller pan (either 2 or 3 inches), the amount of dough and cheese will vary depending on the dimensions of the pan. There are a seemingly infinite variety of sizes for sheet pans, but the chart on page 15 lists the most commonly found sizes. If you possess a pan that does not conform to these sizes, use the information in the chart to make a best guess estimate as to whether to increase or decrease the amount of dough and cheese you need.

PANNING AND DIMPLING

1 Oil the pan, using 1½ tablespoons olive oil, or half oil, half melted butter, for a 9 by 9-inch pan.

2 Place the appropriate size piece of dough in the center of the oiled pan. Rub the surface of the dough with olive oil and use your fingertips to begin dimpling and expanding it in all directions.

3 Cover the pan loosely with plastic wrap and let the dough relax at room temperature for approximately 20 minutes.

4 At 20-minute intervals, dimple from the center, with fingers angled toward the edges and corners. Each successive dimpling will expand the coverage over more of the pan.

5 By the third or fourth dimpling, the dough will evenly cover the whole surface of the pan.

WHY DO YOU PUT HALF OF THE CHEESE ON THE DOUGH BEFORE IT RISES AND THE OTHER HALF JUST BEFORE BAKING?

This is my own innovation and not the way it is done at any pizzeria or restaurant except for one, Mash'd, in Frisco, Texas, where I created this technique with Mash'd Operations Manager Shane Lambert, who asked me what would happen if we put half the cheese on the dough before the final rise. We decided there was only one way to find out, so we tried it. Not only did this extra step tenderize the dough, but it also enhanced the overall flavor. It was so successful that we made it part of the method. It was a breakthrough moment, as you will see when you try it.

- For the deep-pan pizza method in this book, unlike those found in recipes on the web or in other books, the total cheese (cut into cubes, not shredded or grated) is applied in two stages, with half going on before the dough rises (so that it becomes embedded in the dough), and the other half is applied just prior to baking.

- The amount of dough and cheese remains the same whether the pans are 2 or 3 inches deep (but do not use 1-inch pans for this style or the cheese and toppings will ooze out of the pan and into your oven).

- The amount of olive oil (or oil and melted butter combo) used to grease the pans will vary from 1 tablespoon up to 3 tablespoons, depending on the size of pan used.

PAN SIZE	DOUGH WEIGHT	TOTAL CHEESE WEIGHT
6" by 6"	5 ounces / 142 g	4 ounces / 113 g
8" by 8"	8 ounces / 227 g	6 ounces / 170 g
9" by 9"	10 ounces / 284 g	7.5 ounces / 213 g
9" by 13"	14 ounces / 397 g	10 ounces / 284 g
8" by 10"	10 ounces / 284 g	7.5 ounces / 213 g
10" by 14"	16 ounces / 454 g	12 ounces / 340 g
6" round	4 ounces / 113 g	3 ounces / 85 g
8" round	6.5 ounces / 184 g	4.5 ounces / 128 g
9" round	8 ounces / 227 g	6 ounces / 170 g
10" round	9.5 ounces / 269 g	7 ounces / 198 g

CHAPTER 1

IT'S ALL ABOUT THE CRUST

Let's get this out of the way: when it comes to pizza—any kind of pizza really, but especially the kind we're going to make in this book—the bottom line is that it's all about the crust. Some people might say it's also about the sauce or maybe the cheese, and yes, of course, pizza does rely on these, but for great pizza it always comes down to the crust. I'm not referring to good pizza, of which there is plenty in this world. This book is not about good pizza; pizza is such a perfect food that, unless you burn it, it is nearly impossible to screw it up. What this book is about is great pizza.

What is the difference between good and great when it comes to pizza? This begs the deeper question: what is the definition of greatness? In an earlier book, *American Pie*, I explored this very question, and to save you many pages of reading, I can tell you that great pizza, as I define it, always, always, always has a memorable crust. In the fifteen years since that book appeared, there are now many more pizzerias producing memorable pizza, but the same principle applies: the crust is always exquisite.

What do I mean by exquisite? Well, first there is the taste, in which the pizza maker has accomplished the primary mission of all bread bakers: to evoke the full potential of flavor trapped in the grain. This is done by proper adherence to the craft of dough fermentation, the mysterious balancing act of time, temperature, and ingredients that allows the natural sweetness of the wheat (or any other grains for that matter) to emerge through a natural chemical and

biological process. But flavor alone is not the sole memorable quality. There is also texture and an ineffable quality that is often referred to as "snap," which is produced in your mouth as well as in your auditory canals. It is a sound so delightful that, beyond the flavor of the pizza, it induces an undeniable and inexpressible state of joy and inner satisfaction. I call this the sound of crust.

Like a crusty baguette, or a fine piece of toffee, or a crunchy slice of toast, biting into a perfectly made pan pizza fills the mouth with buttery shards and the ears with a musical crackle. It creates a taste-sound association that forever haunts us and a longing that resonates deep within, leaving an indelible taste memory.

This satisfaction is one factor in pan pizza's recent meteoric rise to a level of popularity we must call, for lack of a better word, hotness. Pan pizza is the hottest subcategory within the larger pizza universe. There is a reason for this, I believe, and it is because, when properly made—which you will be able to do when you follow the given instructions—it produces that memorable sound of crust to a greater extent than any other form of pizza, even a perfectly executed Neapolitan Margherita served piping hot from a 900°F wood-fired oven (the pizza that to many people serves as the iconic benchmark of memorable greatness). What's more, and to all of our benefit, a pan pizza doesn't require a wood-fired oven or any other special tools; it can be made in a home oven and still achieve that taste memory and that sound for which we all yearn.

There are many existing, published recipes for the crusts associated with each of the pan-pizza subcategories, but the recipes that follow are, in my opinion, the best of the best, the distillation

---

The pizza's undercrust should caramelize to a rich golden brown, and taste like hot buttered toast.

HIGH-GLUTEN FLOUR

If you like working with high-gluten flour (popular among New York-style pizza makers) because of the extra spring it provides, for the dough formulas in this book, I suggest bumping up the oil to 8 percent of the flour weight instead of the 5 percent that the bread-flour formulas call for, in order to tenderize the texture. Conversely, you can reduce the oil to 3 percent of the flour weight if using all-purpose or Italian double zero flour. But all of these options are very flexible and will require you to experiment a bit to find the sweet spot that works for you.

of the knowledge I've gained and the hard work of re-creating the best pizza crusts I've ever had. They derive from all that I've learned over the past thirty years from the artisan-bread community, which has provided both professional and amateur bakers the necessary knowledge of dough science to truly fulfill what I consider to be the baker's mission: to evoke the full potential of flavor trapped in the grain. The artisan-bread community has now leavened the much larger pizza community, where intuition has often ruled but has been supplemented and reinforced by artisan methodology. As you will see, I've created three distinct dough recipes, or master formulas. They are all interchangeable according to your tastes and preferences. They are: White Flour Dough, Whole Grain Country-Style Dough, and Naturally Leavened Dough (aka sourdough or wild yeast dough).

From these master formulas you can ultimately create your own dough variations, mixing and matching as you see fit, though I suggest you first

master them as shown before developing your own hybrids. Each type of dough can also be used for other styles of non-pan pizzas, such as flatbreads, Neapolitan, and the many other spokes of that universal pizza wheel. But the focus of this book will be on baking world-class, memorable pan pizzas in your home (or pizzeria) ovens. Anything else you choose to do with these formulas, such as baking loaves of bread or making garlic rolls, is a bonus.

THREE MASTER DOUGH FORMULAS

It all starts with the dough, and I'll be the first to admit that there are many ways to make great pizza dough. I've been making pizza and bread dough for over thirty years and have seen nearly every variation imaginable. But, in the end, dough is just flour, water, salt, oil (sometimes), and leaven. Can you add sugar, milk, eggs, and other enrichments? Sure. But after applying every artisan-bread technique within my arsenal, the following three master formulas emerged as the most versatile and most perfect for making all of the styles of pan pizza in this book.

Note that I refer to them as formulas and not just as recipes. A formula indicates that the quantities are determined in some form of relationship, or ratio, to each other. In this case, according to what we call "baker's math," the total flour weight is considered to be the equivalent of 100 percent, and all the other ingredients are calculated as a proportion of that weight. This baker's-formula system allows you to expand or decrease the size

---

Three doughs, from the top: Whole-Grain Country-Style Dough (25 percent whole wheat flour), Naturally Leavened Dough (10 percent wheat flour), and White Flour Dough (100 percent unbleached bread flour).

of any batch by staying within the ratios of the formula. It also enables an experienced baker to immediately identify the type and characteristics of the dough based on its percentage of water (hydration), enrichments (oil or fat, sugar, milk, eggs, etc.), salt, and yeast (or natural sourdough leaven). Though it's not necessary to understand baker's math to make great dough, many bread and pizza enthusiasts want to know how the professionals do it, so I am including the formula ratio percentages in addition to a specific recipe that makes approximately 38 ounces (1.08 kg) of dough. This is exactly the amount needed for one sheet pan (12 by 17 inches) of focaccia pizza, and more than enough for a full pan of Roman-style, Sicilian-style, or Grandma, or two medium-size deep-pan pizzas. In instances where you don't need the full amount of dough, you can save the excess to make a smaller additional pie, or you can chill or freeze the unused piece for baking later.

The Stretch-and-Fold Technique

Another thing that differentiates these doughs is the kneading technique I use. The stretch-and-fold technique is a kneading alternative used by many artisan bakers as a way to strengthen the gluten structure of a dough with minimum mixing time. While mixing is necessary, too much mixing can cause the gluten to over-organize, which creates even, medium-size holes in the baked product, rather than the large, irregular holes favored by artisan bakers. Long mixing also works air into the dough, which reduces flavor and aroma. Short mixing followed by a series of stretch and folds organizes and strengthens the dough without working air into it, as each stretch and fold is equal in function to about a minute of mixing in a machine. The intervals between stretch and folds can be as short as seconds or as long as 45 to 60 minutes, depending on how much fermentation you want to generate before refrigerating the dough. My experience is that three to four stretch-and-fold intervals of 5 minutes each is ideal for pizza dough; the dough will continue to ferment for a while. Once the dough cools down to 39°F in the fridge, the yeast will, essentially, go dormant.

A Test for Gluten Development

It typically takes 5 to 8 minutes for gluten to develop once the flour is hydrated and you begin mixing. Bakers love to pinch off a small piece of dough and gently pull and stretch it to see if it holds together and forms a paper-thin translucent membrane. We call this the "windowpane."

1 Flatten the coarse dough with oiled hands. Use a plastic scraper, or your hands, and lift one end of the dough, folding it to the center.

2 Lift the opposite end and flip it over the folded end.

3 Fold the two wide ends in the same manner, to make the dough into a loose ball.

4 Flip the dough over so that the smooth side is up. Let the dough rest for up to 5 minutes, flatten the dough again with oiled hands, and repeat the folding sequence three more times. By the fourth stretch and fold, the dough will become much smoother and the gluten will be fully developed.

If the dough can hold the membrane, then it means the gluten has developed. Interestingly, though, you don't have to continually mix the dough to develop the gluten; you merely have to hydrate it with water or other liquids and wait for it to happen. The mixing, however, helps the developing gluten to organize itself into a network of strands that ultimately provide the crumb of the baked dough. This is why the stretch-and-fold technique can replace much of the mixing time because, during the rest intervals, the gluten is still developing and the stretching and folding helps organize it further. For these recipes, if you want to do the windowpane test as an exercise in seeing how the gluten develops, do a test before each stretch and fold and see how much stronger the dough gets by the final stretch and fold.

Speeding Up the Process

The use of an already prepared or pre-fermented dough is a way of manipulating time by quantum aging the final dough via the addition of an already fermented piece of older dough. This is a great way to improve flavor and texture, especially in a dough that is mixed and baked on the same day, which is what most bakeries (and some pizzerias) do. These pre-ferments are sometimes a wet, sticky sponge, such as a French-style *poolish*, which is made with equal parts flour and water by weight, with just a pinch of yeast but no salt, or an Italian pre-ferment called *biga*, which is usually a stiffer piece of dough with a small amount of yeast and no salt. But the method described in this book uses cold fermentation (retarding the fermentation of the dough in the refrigerator) to slow down the process, allowing natural enzyme activity to positively affect the flavor and the performance (even without any preferment) of the dough in much the same way that adding old dough (a pre-ferment) to new dough does. While some pizzerias are now using a combination of pre-ferments and retarding to really stretch out the aging process, I've found that the doughs in this book are at peak performance between 18 to 48 hours, with very little discernible difference during this time frame, and can work nicely even up to 72 hours to 96 hours (but I think with less golden coloring and a slightly yeasty taste that some people—though not me—like).

WHOLE GRAIN FLOUR

While I believe that the ideal ratio is 75 percent bread flour and 25 percent whole grain flour for what I call a country dough, I am never opposed to working with a higher ratio of whole grain flour. The main thing to know is that whole grain flour, such as whole wheat or whole rye, absorbs more water than white flour, so the more whole grain flour you add the more water you will need. A general guideline is that for every 2 ounces of whole grain flour you swap in, you will need approximately 0.5 ounce (1 tablespoon or 14 grams) of additional water. You can also add a little honey or sugar to the dough (2 to 3 percent of the flour weight) to sweeten up the bitterness of the bran, but this is totally optional.

Windowpane test of White Flour Dough. Note the threads of gluten holding it together to create a translucent membrane.

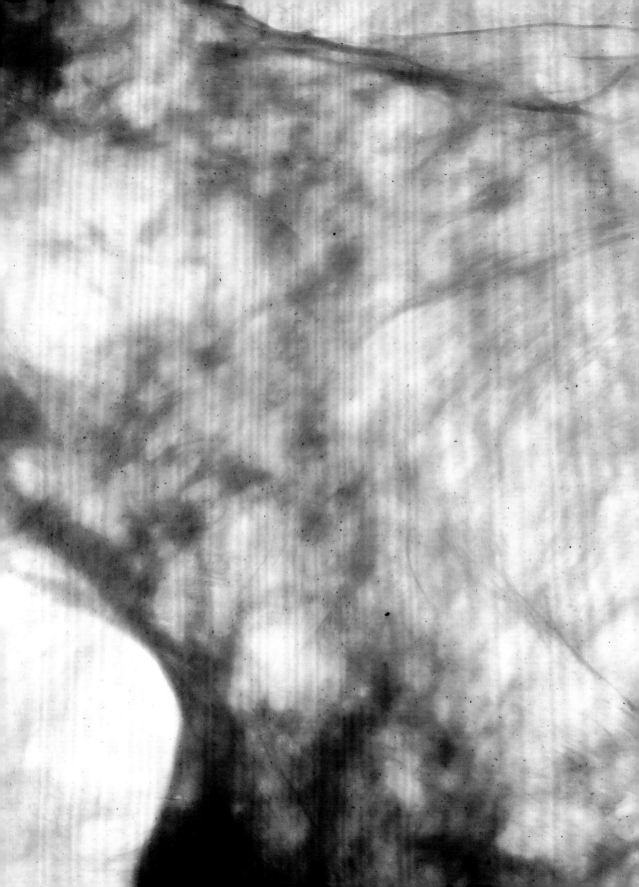

WHITE FLOUR DOUGH

This first dough, which makes a 100 percent white flour pizza crust, is the most popular, but the ones that follow, Whole Grain Country-Style Dough (page 29), with variable amounts of whole grain flour, and Naturally Leavened Dough (page 33) are growing in popularity as interest in whole grain and sourdough baking increases. My suggestion is to first master this white flour dough and then branch out and try the others.

Note that the formula specifically calls for unbleached bread flour and not Italian double zero flour or all-purpose or high-gluten flour (see box, page 20), though you are free to use these, and adjust the hydration as needed, if you wish.

Since the dough requires at least 12 hours of chilling, I recommend making the dough at least 1 day ahead. On the day you plan to bake, follow the steps according to the type of pizza you are making.

VOLUME	OUNCES	GRAMS	INGREDIENT	%
4⅓ cup	1 lb. 4 oz.	567 g	Unbleached bread flour	100
1¾ teaspoons	0.39 oz.	11 g	Kosher salt	1.95
1¼ teaspoons	0.14 oz.	4 g	Instant yeast	0.70
2 cups	16 oz.	454 g	Water, cool (about 60°F)	80
2 tablespoons	1 oz.	28 g	Olive oil	5
1 tablespoon	0.50 oz.	14 g	Extra olive oil (for stretching and folding)	

In the bowl of a stand mixer fitted with the paddle attachment, or in a large mixing bowl, combine the flour, salt, and yeast. Add all of the water and mix on slow speed for 30 seconds or stir with a large spoon to form a coarse, shaggy dough. Add the 2 tablespoons of oil, increase the speed to medium (or continue mixing with the spoon or with wet hands), and mix for another 30 to 60 seconds to make a wet, coarse, sticky dough. It may seem too wet to form a cohesive dough at this stage. Let the dough rest for 5 minutes to fully hydrate.

Increase the mixer speed to medium-high (or continue mixing by hand) and mix for another 30 to 60 seconds to make a smooth, sticky dough. It should be soft, supple, and sticky to the touch, and offer a little resistance when pressed with a wet finger.

CONTINUED >

Use 1 teaspoon of the extra oil to make a 15-inch-diameter oil slick (see page 31) on the work surface. Rub some oil on a plastic bowl scraper and on your hands and use the scraper to transfer the dough to the oil slick. Stretch and fold the dough as shown on page 22. Cover the dough with a bowl and let it rest for 2 to 5 minutes. Repeat the stretch and fold (rub more oil on the work surface as needed), cover the dough, and let it rest for 2 to 5 minutes. Then repeat the stretch and fold, cover with the bowl, and again let it rest for 2 to 5 minutes. Perform a fourth and final stretch and fold to make a smooth ball of dough. The dough will have firmed up after each stretch and fold and will now be soft, smooth, supple, and somewhat sticky but firm enough to hold together when lifted. Transfer the dough to a lightly oiled bowl, cover with plastic wrap, and refrigerate for 12 to 72 hours.

Pan the dough on the day you plan to bake your pizzas (or on the day before, see page 12). If making focaccia, Sicilian-style, Grandma, or Roman-style pizza, follow the instructions for panning on page 139. For deep-pan pizza, weigh and divide the dough according to the size of your pans and follow the instructions for panning on page 15.

WHAT EXACTLY DOES THE TERM COARSE, SHAGGY DOUGH MEAN?

During the early stages of mixing, while the flour is absorbing the liquid (aka hydrating), the dough appears coarse and almost lumpy (see photo, page 26). The more it mixes, the smoother it gets. This coarse appearance is referred to as shaggy, as in the look of a shag rug. Not only will additional mixing smooth it out, but so will the stretching and folding. In my mixing method, it's important to get the dough to the shaggy stage during the first minute of mixing, before briefly kicking up the speed to medium (or, if mixing by hand, to increase the intensity of the kneading or stirring). Once the dough becomes somewhat smoother, you can move on to stretching and folding.

WHOLE GRAIN COUNTRY-STYLE DOUGH

Many of us say we want to eat more whole grain but, when it comes to pizza, the classic white dough almost always seems to win out. However, adding a small amount of whole grain flour, whether whole wheat, rye, or even cornmeal or others, contributes a more complex, earthy flavor without making the crust seem heavy or dense. Country-style French breads typically use anywhere from 10 to 20 percent whole grain flour to 80 to 90 percent white flour, and you can certainly use this ratio for great pizza. But, I found that the magic number for an excellent pizza crust that really feels like it's featuring the whole grain and not just tipping its hat, is 25 percent whole grain flour to 75 percent white flour. Of course, if you really want to push the envelope, you can go all the way up to 100 percent whole grain. If you choose to do so, be aware that whole grain flour, such as whole wheat or whole rye, absorbs more water than white flour, so the more whole grain flour you add, the more water you will need. A general guideline is that for every 2 ounces of whole grain flour you swap in, you will need approximately 0.5 ounce (1 tablespoon or 14 grams) of additional water.

For those who would like to bake with more whole grain, I have included a number of whole grain flour options in the formula, including sprouted whole wheat flour. If you are interested in baking with whole grain flour, sprouted wheat is the flour of the future, and now, at long last, it is available at many supermarkets. For more on this topic see my book *Bread Revolution,* and the Resources section (page 175).

You can also add a little honey or sugar to the dough to sweeten up the bitterness of the bran, but after a lot of experimentation, I determined that the dough for these pizzas is better off without the added sugar, because it will take longer to achieve good browning (caramelization) in the oven. If the crust caramelizes too quickly, before the interior of the dough is fully baked, the crust softens, and the full potential of flavor is not realized. By omitting sugar or honey, we can still bake at a very high setting (500°F, or 450°F for convection) but without caramelizing the crust too early. However, if you like a sweeter taste in your whole grain dough, feel free to add 2 to 3 percent sugar or honey (as a ratio against the flour) and reduce the baking temperature by about 25°F.

CONTINUED >

VOLUME	OUNCES	GRAMS	INGREDIENT	%
3 ¼ cups	15 oz.	425 g	Unbleached bread flour	75
1 cup plus 1 tablespoon	5 oz.	142 g	Whole wheat or sprouted whole wheat flour (or whole rye flour or any other combination of whole grains, such as coarse cornmeal, oat flour, whole spelt, or einkorn flour, etc.)	25
1 ¾ teaspoons	0.39 oz.	11 g	Kosher salt	1.95
1 tablespoon	0.65 oz.	18 g	Honey (optional)	3
1 ¼ teaspoons	0.14 oz.	4 g	Instant yeast	0.70
2 cups plus 2 tablespoons	17 oz.	482 g	Water, cool (approx. 60°F)	80
2 tablespoons plus 1 teaspoon	1.25 oz.	35 g	Olive oil	5.50
1 tablespoon	0.50 oz.	14 g	Extra olive oil (for stretching and folding)	

In the bowl of a stand mixer fitted with the paddle attachment, or in a large mixing bowl, combine the bread flour, whole wheat flour, salt, honey (if using), and yeast. Add all of the water and mix on slow speed for 30 seconds or stir with a large spoon to form a coarse, shaggy dough. Add the 2 tablespoons plus 1 teaspoon of oil, increase the speed to medium (or continue mixing with the spoon or with wet hands), and mix for another 30 to 60 seconds to make a wet, coarse, sticky dough. It may seem too wet to form a cohesive dough at this stage. Let the dough rest for 5 minutes to fully hydrate.

Increase the mixer speed to medium-high (or continue mixing by hand) and mix for another 30 to 60 seconds to make a smooth, sticky dough. It should be soft, supple, and sticky to the touch, and offer a little resistance when pressed with a wet finger.

Use 1 teaspoon of the extra oil to make a 15-inch-diameter oil slick on the work surface. Rub some oil on a plastic bowl scraper and on your hands and use the scraper to transfer the dough to the oil slick. Stretch and fold the dough (see page 22). Cover the dough with a bowl and let it rest for 2 to 5 minutes. Repeat the stretch and fold (rub more oil on the work surface as needed), cover the dough, and let it rest for 2 to 5 minutes. Then repeat the stretch and fold, cover with the bowl, and again let it rest for 2 to 5 minutes. Perform a fourth and final stretch and fold to make a smooth ball of dough. The dough will have firmed up after each stretch and fold and will now be soft, smooth, supple, and somewhat sticky but firm enough to hold together when lifted. Transfer the dough to a lightly oiled bowl, cover with plastic wrap, and refrigerate for 12 to 72 hours.

Pan the dough on the day you plan to bake your pizzas. If making focaccia, Sicilian-style, Grandma, or Roman-style pizza, follow the instructions for panning on page 12. For deep-pan pizza, weigh and divide the dough according to the size of your pans and follow the instructions for panning on page 15.

I recommend making the dough 1 day ahead. On the day you plan to bake, follow the steps according to the type of pizza you are making.

WHAT IS AN OIL SLICK?

The oil slick is a trick to make dough handling easier, especially the stretch-and-fold technique. You simply wipe the work surface with a small amount of oil, about 1 teaspoon (olive or vegetable), to create a nonstick surface for the dough. The oil slick has very little impact on flavor or texture, because it comprises such a small amount of oil, but any impact it does have is positive.

NATURALLY LEAVENED DOUGH

Naturally leavened sourdough (aka wild yeast dough) is the ultimate frontier for bread bakers, as it requires much more skill and craft than baking with the more predictable commercial yeast. It is growing in popularity because of its flavor but also because recent research indicates that naturally fermented dough, especially if fermented over a long period of time, is easier to digest and may be safer for people with wheat or gluten sensitivities (but not for those with celiac disease, about 1.3 percent of the population).

Making your own sourdough starter requires a little time and patience but is not difficult, nor is it difficult to maintain the starter with periodic feedings (the addition of flour and water), as you will see on page 36. The following formula presupposes that you already have a sourdough starter ready to deploy. If not, see the following section for a primer on sourdough cultivation and care.

Sourdough purists prefer to leave out commercial yeast altogether, but I believe there are a couple advantages to adding a small amount of instant yeast (aka "spiking the dough"). One reason is that the dough will rise at a slightly faster pace than if using only sourdough starter as your leaven. Without the yeast, it could take anywhere from 5 to 8 hours during the primary fermentation and 4 to 6 hours during the final rise (in the pan). With the added yeast, the rises should take about one-half to two-thirds of that time. Also, the longer the rising cycles, the more acidic the dough will taste, possibly competing too much with the other pizza flavors. Of course, if you prefer a very tangy sourdough, feel free to omit the yeast and factor in the additional fermentation times.

After you've mastered this formula, you can experiment with substituting whole grain flour for some or all of the bread flour, as noted in the chart for Whole Grain Country-Style Dough on page 29.

CONTINUED >

Making an oil slick.

VOLUME	OUNCES	GRAMS	INGREDIENT	%
4 cups	18 oz.	510 g	Unbleached bread flour	100
1 ¾ teaspoons	0.45 oz.	13 g	Kosher salt	2.55
2 teaspoons	0.50 oz.	14 g	Sugar (optional; will make a tangier starter)	2.80
1 teaspoon	0.11 oz.	3 g	Instant yeast (optional)	0.60
1 cup	6 oz.	170 g	Sourdough starter (see page 36)	33
1 ¾ cups plus 1 tablespoon	14.50 oz.	411 g	Water, cool (approx. 60°F)	80
2 tablespoons	1 oz.	28 g	Olive or vegetable oil	5.50
1 tablespoon	0.50 oz.	14 g	Extra oil (for stretching and folding)	

In the bowl of a stand mixer fitted with the paddle attachment, or in a large mixing bowl, combine the flour, salt, and the sugar and the instant yeast, if using. Add the sourdough starter and the water and mix on slow speed for 30 seconds or stir with a large spoon to form a coarse, shaggy dough. Add the 2 tablespoons of oil, increase the speed to medium (or continue mixing with the spoon or with wet hands), and mix for another 30 to 60 seconds to make a wet, sticky dough. It may seem too wet to form a cohesive dough at this stage. Let the dough rest for 5 minutes to fully hydrate.

Increase the mixer speed to medium-high (or continue mixing by hand) and mix for another 30 to 60 seconds to make a smooth, sticky dough. It should be soft, supple, and sticky to the touch, and offer a little resistance when pressed with a wet finger.

Use 1 teaspoon of the extra oil to make a 15-inch-diameter oil slick on the work surface. Rub some oil on a plastic bowl scraper and on your hands and use the scraper to transfer the dough to the oil slick. Stretch and fold the dough as shown on page 22. Cover the dough with a bowl and let it rest for 2 to 5 minutes. Repeat the stretch and fold (rub more oil on the work surface if needed), cover the dough, and let it rest for 2 to 5 minutes. Then repeat the stretch and fold, cover with the bowl, and again let it rest for another 2 to 5 minutes. Perform a fourth and final stretch and fold to make a smooth ball of dough. The dough will have firmed up after each stretch and fold and will now be soft, smooth, supple, and somewhat sticky but firm enough to hold together when lifted.

Transfer the dough to a lightly oiled bowl and cover with plastic wrap. If using yeast, immediately place the bowl in the refrigerator to retard the dough overnight or for up to 3 days. The dough will take roughly the same amount of time to rise as both the white flour and country-style doughs. However, if using starter only, let the dough ferment at room temperature for 4 to 6 hours, or until it increases one and one-half times in size. (Once the dough has risen and been retarded, allow 2 to 5 additional hours for the fully panned dough to rise to the appropriate size.) The time will depend on the strength of your starter and the temperature of the room.

Stretch and fold the dough to deflate it and return it to the bowl. Cover and refrigerate to slowly ferment overnight or for up to 3 days. You can also weigh and pan a piece of dough in a prepared sheet pan for whatever type of pizza you are making. This dough can then be refrigerated for anywhere from 12 to 72 hours.

If making focaccia, Grandma, Sicilian-style or Roman-style pizza, follow the instructions for panning on page 139. For deep-pan pizza, weigh and divide according to the size of your pans and follow the instructions for panning on page 15. On the day you plan to bake, follow the steps according to the type of pizza you are making.

THE CARE AND FEEDING
OF A SOURDOUGH STARTER

Sourdough starters, which are the oldest method of leavening dough, should more properly be called natural or wild yeast starters because not all versions of this method produce sour-tasting bread (the French, for instance, refer to natural starter as levain, and think of the tart American sourdough as "spoiled bread"). Natural starters are biologically very complex, and many books have been dedicated to explaining the science of wild yeast natural starters. In this section, however, I will simply provide some basics as well as a proven method for making a sourdough starter and keeping it alive for ongoing use. You can find more detailed information in my previous books, *The Bread Baker's Apprentice*, *Bread Revolution*, or *Artisan Bread Everyday*, as well as in many other fine bread books and other resources (see page 175). In the meantime, here are some key things to know:

The general scientific term for wild yeast is *Saccharomyces exiguous* (as opposed to commercially produced dry or fresh yeast, which is cultivated from a specific strain called *Saccharomyces cerevisiae*). But the Latin word *exiguous* simply means "wild," and there are many strains of wild yeast, depending on where you live and where the wheat was grown or milled, so exiguous is a very broad term, and the strains can vary from place to place.

The sour, or acidic, flavor notes of this dough are created not by the wild yeast itself but by the fermentation of many strains of bacteria. The most famous of these, from a baker's perspective, is one called *lactobacillus sanfranciscensis*, which produces a tangy, lactic acid flavor that Americans, especially those living in, where else, the San Francisco Bay Area, love. Recent studies have shown that this strain is not exclusive to the Bay Area and actually exists throughout the world.

As with wild yeast, many bacterial strains, dependent on the climate, water, and soil of their locales, have their own flavor influence on dough that is fermented with natural starters.

A natural sourdough starter can be made with many types of flour and there are dozens, perhaps hundreds, of different methods for making starters, each producing distinct flavor nuances. However, once a starter is established (which can take anywhere from 7 to 14 days) and put on a feeding schedule, it will eventually develop a flavor profile influenced by the flour you feed it as well as by the region in which you live. In other words, you can make sourdough starters anywhere in the world and, while they may each be different from starters produced elsewhere, they all contain the requisite wild yeast and bacteria to ferment dough and cause it to rise. The bottom line: A starter is a type of pre-fermented dough in which various strains of wild yeast and bacteria coexist, all searching for food (glucose mainly) and digesting it to produce carbon dioxide, alcohol, and various types of lactic and acetic acids.

HOW TO MAKE A STARTER

For those of you just starting out in this wonderful, seemingly intimidating world of sourdough, here is an easy method that will produce a starter within 7 to 10 days (14 at most). It is followed by instructions for keeping it alive and refreshed for years to come (the Boudin Sourdough Company in San Francisco, for instance, claims to have kept their starter alive since 1849).

If you are already an experienced baker and have a sourdough "mother" starter in your repertoire, you need simply to feed it at 80 percent hydration (water to flour) to make it user friendly for the sourdough pizza crusts in this book. You can also use it as is and simply adjust the final dough hydration, as needed, to achieve a total water-to-flour ratio of 80 percent.

I am suggesting the use of pineapple or orange juice as the liquid on Day 1 because the acidity in the juice helps shorten the time to get the process started, in other words, to jump-start the starter, if you will. Wild yeast cells prefer a somewhat acidic pH in which to grow, and there are some bacteria that mimic yeast activity at more neutral pH levels, fooling us into thinking the starter is ready before it actually is. The juice is not required, as the starter will work with just water if you are patient, but it has become a trusted method.

Day 1

In a glass or stainless-steel bowl, combine 1 cup (4.5 ounces/128 g) of flour, either unbleached bread flour or whole wheat, with 3.5 ounces (99 g) pineapple juice, orange juice, or cool or room-temperature water.

Stir the flour and liquid together to make a wet, sticky dough (similar in structure to the pizza dough on page 27). Use a rubber spatula to scrape all the dough on the interior sides back into the bowl. Cover the bowl loosely with plastic wrap or a lid and leave at room temperature for approximately 24 hours.

Day 2

Stir the dough with a large spoon for about 30 seconds to aerate it and redistribute the ingredients. There should be little or no fermentation activity at this point. Again, leave covered at room temperature for another 24 hours.

Day 3

There may or may not be any signs of fermentation or bubbling, but regardless, mix 1 cup of unbleached bread flour and 3.5 ounces (99 g) of water at room temperature into the dough and stir for about 60 seconds with a large spoon or rubber spatula to form a smooth dough. Again, scrape down any dough on the interior sides back into the dough (dough on the sides can dry out and become crusty as well as being more vulnerable to mold-forming bacteria). Cover

CONTINUED >

loosely with plastic wrap or a lid and leave at room temperature for 8 hours. Then, stir the dough again to aerate it, cover it as before, and leave it at room temperature.

Day 4 and After

There is a good likelihood that the dough will show some signs of fermentation (bubbling, alcohol or buttermilk or acidic aromas, expansion in size). Even if it doesn't, mix in another 1 cup of unbleached bread flour and 3.5 ounces (99 g) of water, scraping the dough on the interior sides back into the dough. Cover loosely and leave at room temperature. You're done with feeding but continue to stir twice a day until the dough comes to life, actively fermenting, creating bubbles, and doubling in size. It should develop a pleasant, acidic aroma, similar to that of apple cider. This could take anywhere from 1 to 8 days, depending on your climate, the time of year, and the ambient temperature of your kitchen; a few degrees' difference can affect the rate of this initial fermentation development by as many as 3 or 4 days. If there is little or no activity during the initial few days, do not give up on it. The frequent stirring will prevent it from getting moldy and encourage the growth of the right kind of microorganisms.

When the starter bubbles to life and doubles in size (or rises and falls), immediately stir to deflate the dough, cover it more tightly, and refrigerate it. It is now ready to use and will become the mother starter from which future pizza dough as well as bread dough can be made.

HOW TO REFRESH YOUR STARTER

Once a mother starter has been unused for more than 5 days, it begins to break down. In such cases, the dough will become soupy and lose its structural integrity, but the microorganisms within are still viable albeit dormant. If you use it, as is, in your final dough, it will weaken the structure, so it must first be refreshed. The easiest way to refresh a starter is by simply adding more flour and water to it at the same 77 to 80 percent hydration ratio as in the beginning and at any volume you choose. For a starter that has been unused for 5 to 10 days, my preference is to build it by adding flour at double the weight of the starter. For example, if you have 8 ounces (227 g) of old starter, you would add 16 ounces (454 g) of bread flour plus 12.8 ounces (363 g) of water and then allow about 4 to 8 hours for it to ferment and become a new, stronger mother starter, weighing about 2.25 pounds. Note: You can also discard all but 4 ounces and begin rebuilding it from there, by adding 8 ounces flour and 6.5 ounces of water. This will, after a few hours of fermentation, turn into about 18 ounces of refreshed mother starter.

However, in instances where the mother starter hasn't been used for 10 days or more, I prefer to

CONTINUED >

From Day 1 (left) to final mother starter, approximately 5 to 9 days later

refresh it at a ratio of four times the amount of flour to starter because the original mother starter is overly compromised and needs more new flour for the refreshment. In instances like this, it might also take longer for the newly refreshed starter to ferment, perhaps 6 to 12 hours, so you have to plan accordingly. Also, feeding it at this ratio can quickly gobble up a lot of flour and produce more mother starter than you need (unless making large batches of pizza dough or bread). So, it might be better to weigh out a small amount of this old mother starter, say 2 ounces (57 g), and add 8 ounces (227 g) of flour plus 6.5 ounces (184 g) of water (approximately 80 percent of the flour weight). This will produce about 1 pound of new starter, which is probably enough for most home bakers, since you only need 6 ounces of starter in your single-batch recipes. In fact, if your mother starter is fresh and strong, you could make 2 or more batches of sourdough crust with it and still retain 4 to 6 ounces for refreshing it when the time comes. (Note: When pulling out a small amount of old starter to make a new mother starter, hold on to the remaining old starter as insurance or backup, at least until the new mother starter proves itself viable. Once the new starter is up and running, you can discard the old mother starter.)

Don't panic if your sourdough starter or your final pizza dough doesn't rise according to the timetable described in the instructions. There are many factors that can affect the rise of a dough, including the potency of your starter (is it fairly young, has it been refreshed a number of times, did it double in size since the last refreshment, etc.?). Environmental conditions such as room temperature, humidity, and the temperature of your dough are also factors. After you've used your starter in a dough and refreshed it a few times, it should settle into a more predictable fermentation pattern, but the first rule of thumb is to never give up on your starter or your dough if it seems sluggish; just give it more time or find a warmer place (but not the oven set on low, because that's still too hot). You can heat the oven for a few minutes to warm up, then turn it off, using the warm oven as a proof box, but always leave the door propped slightly open just to be sure it doesn't get too warm (the wild yeast and bacteria will die as they approach 138°F). In the end, patience will win out. Remember to keep the dough covered so that it doesn't form a skin or get caught in a draft, which can slow down fermentation. If the dough is very sluggish, it usually means the starter just wasn't at full potency, but still, given a few extra hours, it will eventually raise your dough.

FINAL NOTES

For those who want a more acidic taste, the addition of a small amount of sugar (2 to 3 percent of the flour weight), either when refreshing the starter itself or in the final dough, fosters the development of bacteria that produce flavors that are more acidic. If you prefer a less sour or tangy flavor, use instant yeast in your final dough in addition to the starter to reduce fermentation time and, thus, diminish the development of acid-producing bacteria.

Once your mother starter is established, or refreshed, you should store it in a clean plastic, glass, or ceramic container with a tight-fitting lid or wrap to prevent air from drying the surface or exposing it to extraneous microorganisms in the refrigerator. It's best to use a new or cleaned container after each refreshment. If you are leaving the starter dormant in the refrigerator for weeks or months, just be sure the interior sides of the container are scraped back down into the main dough with a wet rubber spatula.

If you are wondering about keeping a stiffer or wetter sourdough starter in the refrigerator, there really is no rule, since sourdough starters can be kept at many different levels of hydration.

Wet, spongelike starters (equal parts flour and water) are easier to refresh than stiffer starters, but neither is difficult. The advantage of my "rustic starter" (80 percent water to flour) is that it is the same ratio and consistency as the final dough, so it is easy to incorporate without having to adjust the water ratio in the final dough. Instructions for refreshing the sourdough starter using this system follow below.

You can use a refreshed mother starter as your actual starter in the Naturally Leavened Dough recipe (page 33) or, if it has been more than 5 to 7 days since it's last refreshment, use a small amount of the mother starter to build a fresh, final starter at the 2-to-1 ratio (2 parts flour to 1 part starter plus 80 percent water). (If more than 7 to 10 days, use the 4-to-1 flour to starter ratio, as described above.)

Example for a single-batch dough: If you need only 6 ounces (170 g) of starter from a 5-day-old mother starter, you can mix 1.5 ounces (43 g) mother starter, 3 ounces (85 g) flour, and 2.4 ounces (68 g) water. Give it 4 to 6 hours to "ripen" (ferment to double in size) and you'll be good to go.

CHAPTER 2

SAUCES AND SPECIALTY TOPPINGS

There are many ways to make pizza sauce, but I think the best way is also the simplest: use good-quality canned tomatoes (and most store brands are good, even though all cooks have their preference), and then don't fuss with it. I have used the following two tomato pizza sauces, which I introduced in *American Pie: My Search for the Perfect Pizza,* in my consulting work, and I regularly get emails confirming their popularity. I'm tweaking them only slightly for these pizzas, but the key is this: The tomatoes are already cooked when they are put in the can, so there is no need to cook them again in a saucepan as if it were pasta sauce. If the sauce goes on the pizza before the bake, it will get cooked again, and if it's used as a finishing sauce after the pizza comes out of the oven, as in some of the deep-pan and Roman-style pizzas, it will taste so fresh and vibrant that you'll be glad you didn't cook it

on the stove first. They are very easy to make and will keep in the refrigerator for at least a week or two and in the freezer for months.

Also, in a pinch, I have no problem using store-bought pizza or pasta sauce in a jar. While it may not be as fresh or vibrant as homemade sauce, almost every commercial brand is still pretty good and, hey, remember what I wrote earlier: it's all about the crust; the toppings are just a bonus.

In addition to the sauces, there are some specialty toppings here that are worth making and adding to your repertoire. Some are integral to certain pizza recipes in the upcoming chapters. Like some secret ingredients, they can make a huge difference in both flavor and presentation, and they have a long shelf life if kept refrigerated or frozen.

CRUSHED TOMATO PIZZA SAUCE

MAKES ENOUGH FOR 4 TO 8 PIZZAS

Some brands of canned tomatoes are more heavily salted than others, so adjust the flavors at the end, according to your taste. You can use crushed tomatoes (sometimes also labeled ground tomatoes), or you can buy canned whole tomatoes and crush them with your hands or grind them in a food processor. This is my favorite, go-to sauce, as I love the texture of the tomato solids (as opposed to the smooth texture of the following marinara sauce, which I find to be more popular among kids).

One 28-ounce can crushed, ground, or whole tomatoes

¼ teaspoon coarsely ground black pepper

1 teaspoon dried basil, or 2 tablespoons minced fresh basil

¼ teaspoon dried oregano, or 1 teaspoon chopped fresh oregano

1 teaspoon granulated garlic, or 2 large garlic cloves, finely minced, plus more as needed

1 tablespoon red wine vinegar or freshly squeezed lemon juice, or a combination, plus more as needed

½ to 1 teaspoon kosher salt

In a large bowl, stir together the tomatoes, pepper, basil, oregano, garlic, vinegar or lemon juice, and ½ teaspoon of the salt, adding the salt gradually and tasting as you go. Add more vinegar or lemon juice and salt, if needed. But be careful; the flavors of the herbs, garlic, and salt will intensify when the pizza is baked, so resist the urge to increase the amount. You can always add more herbs and salt on top of the pizza after it comes out of the oven.

Transfer to a covered container, seal tightly, and refrigerate up to 10 days or freeze up to 3 months.

ALL-PURPOSE MARINARA PIZZA SAUCE

MAKES ENOUGH FOR 4 TO 8 PIZZAS

This sauce is smoother than the crushed tomato sauce, and it contains more herbs. It can be used on nearly any type of pizza (or pasta) that calls for tomato sauce, and as I said earlier, kids love it!

For this sauce, I call for dried herbs. If you prefer to use fresh herbs, sprinkle them on the pizzas as soon as they come out of the oven. If you do not have thyme or marjoram, you may substitute additional portions of oregano or basil. For a less assertive garlic flavor, omit the granulated or fresh garlic and lightly sauté 8 pressed garlic cloves in olive oil. Then drizzle the garlic and oil over the pizza when it comes out of the oven.

One 28-ounce can tomato puree

8 to 14 ounces water, at room temperature

1 tablespoon dried parsley

2 teaspoons dried basil

½ teaspoon dried oregano

½ teaspoon dried thyme

½ teaspoon dried marjoram (optional)

¼ teaspoon freshly ground black pepper

4 tablespoons olive oil

1 teaspoon granulated garlic, or 2 cloves of garlic, finely minced (or 8 garlic cloves, pressed, and lightly sautéed in olive oil)

2 tablespoons red wine vinegar or freshly squeezed lemon juice

1 to 2 teaspoons kosher salt

In a large bowl, mix together the tomato puree, 8 ounces of the water, the parsley, basil, oregano, thyme, marjoram (if using), pepper, oil, granulated or minced garlic, the vinegar or lemon juice, and 1 teaspoon of the salt. If the sauce is too thick, stir in some or all of the remaining 6 ounces of water. Taste and adjust the seasoning by adding some or all of the remaining salt.

Transfer to a covered container, seal tightly, and refrigerate up to 10 days or freeze for 3 months.

PESTO GENOVESE

When I first discovered pesto about forty years ago, I thought that I had gone to heaven. Pesto was so new and different to Americans then. Sadly, we've now become too familiar with it, and it has been overused in so many ways that now it runs the risk of being a culinary cliché. However, during my travels through Liguria and Genoa, where pesto has been a staple for centuries, I found that nobody seemed to have tired of it. All it took was one dinner there, and my passion for pesto was reborn.

Here in the States, the problem with much of the pesto is its lack of what I would call brightness. Nowadays, a lot of restaurant pesto is a dull green, thick, and pasty, the flavors locked up, trapped in the cheese. Back in the 1970s, pesto was too new to be taken for granted. I tried it for the first time in San Francisco, at Tony La Tona's legendary Caffe Sport. His pesto was bright green, and the basil flavor exploded in my mouth, carried home by the cheese and pine nut base notes. It changed my life.

It had been a long time since pesto had sent me into such ecstasy, but when it was served to me over some toothsome, house-made troffie pasta at da Vittorio in the Ligurian seaside town of Recco, I felt as though time had compressed and I was discovering it anew, just like my first time at Caffe Sport.

I came up with the following recipe to channel those great taste memories. This pesto is smooth and creamy and very spreadable, not thick and pasty. You can use all pine nuts or all walnuts, whichever you prefer or have on hand. If you like to experiment, try a combination of the two. The sauce can be added to a focaccia or pizza just before it goes into the oven or drizzled over it after it comes out.

1 cup pine nuts or walnuts, divided

2 tablespoons olive oil (not extra-virgin)

8 garlic cloves, coarsely chopped

2 cups tightly packed fresh basil leaves (from 2 to 3 large bunches), washed and dried

1 cup extra-virgin olive oil, plus more as needed

2 tablespoons freshly squeezed lemon juice

1 cup freshly grated Parmesan, Romano, or Asiago cheese, divided

Kosher salt, as needed

CONTINUED >

In a dry skillet, lightly toast the nuts over medium heat until they just begin to release their aroma and show signs of browning, 3 to 5 minutes. Immediately transfer them to a bowl and set aside.

In the same skillet, heat the oil over medium-high heat. When the oil is very hot but not smoking, turn off the heat, add the chopped garlic, and stir for about 5 seconds. (The garlic does not need to be browned; the quick cooking is merely to take away the "burn" from the garlic and release its flavor.) Immediately transfer the oil and garlic to an empty bowl and set aside.

Combine the basil, the garlic with oil, the 1 cup of extra-virgin olive oil, half of the toasted nuts, the lemon juice, and ½ cup of the grated cheese in the bowl of a food processor fitted with the metal blade attachment (or in a high-powered blender). Process the ingredients until smooth, adding more oil if needed, and transfer the mixture to a bowl. It should be runny and thin, not thick and stiff.

Slowly fold in the remaining pine nuts and the remaining ½ cup of cheese, stopping before the pesto becomes too thick; it should be thin enough to drizzle. If it is too thick, whisk in a little more oil; if too thin, add more grated cheese. Taste the pesto. If it is undersalted (it probably won't be), add either some salt or a little more cheese.

Transfer the pesto to an airtight container, seal tightly, and store in the refrigerator for about 1 week. Be aware that it will begin to lose some of its bright color the longer it sits.

PESTO VARIATIONS

The following are based on the foregoing basil pesto master recipe and provide alternative flavor and color bases.

PARSLEY PESTO

Substitute an equal amount of flat-leaf parsley for the basil or any combination of parsley and fresh basil equaling 2 cups. This combination is milder in flavor than Pesto Genovese but equally vibrant.

SPINACH PESTO

Replace the basil with 2 cups fresh baby spinach, and process as directed. (You can also use fresh baby kale or baby arugula leaves or a blend of spinach and fresh basil.) You will need ½ teaspoon or more salt. This makes a very bright green pesto.

ROASTED PEPPER PESTO

Substitute an equal amount of roasted red peppers for the basil (or any combination of the two) to make a bright red pesto with rich flavor.

SUN-DRIED TOMATO PESTO

Prepare the basil pesto as directed, but add about 5 marinated sun-dried tomatoes to create more complexity. For a less intense flavor, use oven-roasted tomatoes, which are available at gourmet delis. You can also make your own by brushing tomato slices with Herb Oil (page 54) and roasting them at 400°F for about 20 minutes, or at 175°F overnight.

HERB OIL

I guarantee that you will use this oil more than any other specialty topping, and you can make as much as you like because it will keep indefinitely in the refrigerator. It's used primarily on focaccia, but it is also excellent drizzled over many types of pizza, or as a marinade for various pizza toppings, especially sliced tomatoes and potatoes (see Susan's Rosemary-Garlic Potatoes pizza, page 165). There is an infinite number of ways to make this oil, using both fresh and dried herbs in many different combinations. However, if replacing the granulated garlic with fresh garlic, I recommend using 6 cloves, pressed or chopped and sautéed in ¼ cup olive oil for 3 to 5 seconds, not to brown it but to take out the "burn" and enhance the flavor. So, consider the following recipe merely a starting point until you find your own favorite combination.

1 cup olive oil	½ teaspoon fresh or dried rosemary leaves	½ teaspoon red pepper flakes (optional)
1 tablespoon dried basil	½ teaspoon dried thyme	¼ teaspoon hot or mild paprika (optional)
1 tablespoon dried parsley	1 teaspoons granulated garlic	1 teaspoon kosher salt or coarse sea salt
1 teaspoon dried oregano		

In a bowl, whisk together the oil, basil, parsley, oregano, rosemary, thyme, garlic, and pepper flakes and paprika (if using), gradually adding the salt and whisking the oil to bring the salt to the surface before tasting. Store in the refrigerator in a container with a lid, where it will keep for at least 6 months.

Note: I recommend using whole-leaf dried herbs, not ground herbs. If you'd prefer to use fresh herbs, use three to four times more than the dried herbs by volume, mince them, and stir them into the oil immediately to prevent oxidation.

SPICY OIL

My wife, Susan, and I fell in love with this spicy oil the first time we had it, twenty years ago, at Al Forno in Providence, Rhode Island, and we've been making our own version ever since. This condiment is excellent drizzled over almost any kind of pizza, pasta, or even soup. The following recipe—with a couple of tweaks of our own—is based on the version from the Al Forno founders' cookbook, *Cucina Simpatica.*

1 cup olive oil

1 tablespoon plus 1 teaspoon sweet or hot paprika

1 tablespoon plus 1 teaspoon red pepper flakes

1 large garlic clove, peeled

¼ teaspoon kosher salt or coarse salt

In a saucepan, whisk together the oil, paprika, pepper flakes, garlic, and salt and bring to a boil. Lower the heat and simmer gently for 10 minutes. Then turn off the heat and let the oil cool for 30 minutes.

Strain the oil into a jar and let it cool completely. Cover tightly and refrigerate. It will keep almost indefinitely but for at least up to 6 months.

CARAMELIZED BALSAMIC ONION MARMALADE

MAKES 1½ TO 2 CUPS

This sweet and tangy condiment is one of my favorites, and I like to use it on top of focaccia (see page 129) and pizzas (see page 170). You can never have too much of it in reserve, because it can liven up many other dishes, including sandwiches, and makes a great garnish. It takes about 45 minutes to make, so don't wait until the last minute.

Long, slow cooking will sweeten any onions, so save those Vidalias or Walla Wallas for other uses, such as salads and sandwiches, and use regular yellow or white onions for this recipe.

¼ cup olive or vegetable oil

4 large yellow or white onions, thinly sliced

½ cup sugar

¼ cup balsamic vinegar

¼ teaspoon salt

Pinch of freshly ground black pepper

In a large frying pan or saucepan, heat the oil over medium heat. When the oil is hot, add the onions, lower the heat to medium-low, and sauté, stirring occasionally, for 25 to 30 minutes, or until the onions begin to soften and turn translucent. Do not cook over high heat, as the outside of the onions will char before the interior has softened and sweetened. Continue stirring for another few minutes, until the onions have softened and begin to turn a light amber color. Add the sugar and continue stirring until the sugar melts and begins to bubble. Clear a space in the center of the pan, pour the balsamic vinegar directly into the hot pan, and then stir the onions into the vinegar. Continue stirring for 1 to 2 minutes, until all the onions are coated, and then remove the pan from the heat.

In a mesh strainer set over a clean saucepan, strain the onions, pressing them with a large spoon to release their juice, and wait a few minutes until they stop dripping. Return the strained onions to the saucepan in which they were cooked and set them aside.

Bring the juice to a simmer over medium-high heat, stirring continuously, until thickened. This should take only a few minutes, so don't leave the pan unattended. As soon as the juice thickens into a honeylike syrup, remove it from the heat, pour it all back over the onions, and stir with a rubber spatula until they are coated with the syrup. Stir in the salt and pepper and let the onions cool.

Transfer the mixture to a container, seal tightly, and refrigerate for up to 2 weeks or transfer to sandwich-size resealable freezer bags and freeze for up to 6 months. Defrost at room temperature before using.

CARAMELIZED GARLIC CLOVES AND GARLIC OIL

MAKES 1 TO 1½ CUPS

There are a number of ways to caramelize garlic, but my favorite method is the one that follows, partly because the aroma of the garlic oil is so intoxicating. While not listed as an ingredient in any of the pizzas in this book, this garlic and its oil can be used for practically all of them if, like me, you love the flavor of roasted garlic. There are so many other uses for caramelized garlic, as well as for garlic oil, that I always make large batches and keep the excess on hand in the freezer or refrigerator. Use the oil for salad dressings, stir fries, or bread dipping and, of course, for drizzling over pizza. This duo is also a good substitution for some of the granulated garlic and regular olive oil used to make Herb Oil (page 54). Some folks like to use the soft cloves like butter, spreading them on their pizzas as a condiment.

4 heads of garlic (about 48 cloves), cloves separated and peeled

About 2 cups olive oil

In a small saucepan, combine the garlic cloves and enough oil to completely cover them and bring to a rapid boil over high heat, stirring every 10 to 20 seconds to prevent sticking and burning. Once the oil comes to a boil, reduce the heat to a simmer and continue cooking, gently stirring, until the garlic cloves all turn a rich golden brown over their entire surface, 6 to 8 minutes.

Remove the pan from the heat. Using a slotted spoon or a skimming tool, transfer the garlic to a clean bowl and let cool. Strain off any excess oil that collects in the bowl of garlic and return it to the oil remaining in the saucepan.

When the garlic and oil have cooled, transfer the cloves to a resealable plastic bag and refrigerate for up to 5 days or in the freezer for up to 3 months. Transfer the garlic oil to a container, seal tightly, and refrigerate for up to 3 months.

SECRET SAUCES

The following three pepper relishes range from spicy to mild and can serve as a condiment for many foods. Pairing them with hoagies (aka subs) and pizzas in particular brings out the best in both. I have more to say about the relationship between pizza and hoagies on page 81, but suffice it to say, "secret sauce" is the magical key to many great sandwiches, of which hoagies, as any Philly boy like me knows, are the greatest. The pizzas on pages 75, 81, and 112 capture that same magic, and frankly, any of the following secret sauces will enliven nearly any kind of pizza, so it always pays off to have some on hand. In addition to my own cache of secret sauces, I always keep a jar of Haddon House or Cento Hoagie Spread on hand (available at most supermarkets).

If you prefer a coarse emulsified texture, use a blender to puree these sauces. For a chunkier version, use a food processor fitted with a metal blade and pulse the ingredients until they are broken down and form a coarse but juicy relishlike mash.

SECRET SAUCE 1 (SPICY)

1 cup pickled red cherry peppers, stemmed

1 cup pickled jalapeño peppers, or 3 fresh red or green jalapeño peppers, stemmed but not seeded

¼ cup cherry pepper or jalapeño pepper brine

3 garlic cloves, peeled

1 cup red wine vinegar

1 tablespoon olive oil

¼ teaspoon salt, plus more as needed

Combine the cherry peppers, jalapeños, brine, garlic, vinegar, oil, and ¼ teaspoon salt in a blender or food processor and puree to desired texture. Taste and add more salt, if needed.

Transfer to a covered container or jar, seal tightly, and refrigerate for up to 6 months.

CONTINUED >

SECRET SAUCE 2 (MEDIUM)

1 cup pickled pepperon-
cini peppers, stemmed

¼ cup pepperoncini brine

½ cup pickled red cherry
peppers, stemmed

1 large red bell pepper,
stemmed and seeded

3 garlic cloves

1 cup red wine vinegar

1 tablespoon olive oil

¼ teaspoon salt,
plus more as needed

Combine the pepperoncini peppers, brine, cherry peppers, bell pepper, garlic, vinegar, oil, and ¼ teaspoon salt in a blender or food processor and puree to desired texture. Taste and add more salt, if needed.

Transfer to a covered container or jar, seal tightly, and refrigerate for up to 6 months.

SECRET SAUCE 3 (MILD)

2 large red bell peppers,
stemmed and seeded

1 cup pickled pepperon-
cini peppers

¼ cup pepperoncini brine

3 garlic cloves

1 cup red wine vinegar

1 tablespoon olive oil

¼ teaspoon salt,
plus more as needed

Combine the bell peppers, pepperoncini peppers, brine, garlic, vinegar, oil, and salt in a blender or food processor and puree to desired texture. Taste and add more salt, if needed.

Transfer to a covered container or jar, seal tightly, and refrigerate for up to 6 months.

CHAPTER 3

DEEP-PAN [DETROIT-STYLE] PIZZA

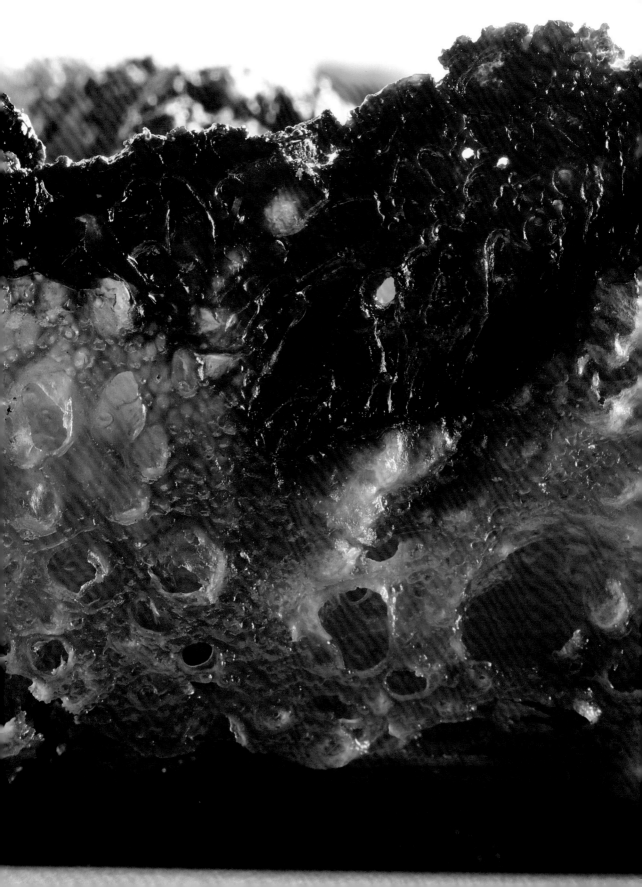

The whole concept of deep-pan pizza is a paean to the notion of more rather than less. While the Neapolitan Margherita pizza is the icon of pizza minimalism, the Detroit-style, aka deep-pan square, is its polar opposite. It's way too much cheese, way too much dough, way too much oil, but also way too good to stop eating it. Like the Chicago-style deep-dish (but even better, some like me would argue), it is pizza as indulgence. It is, figuratively speaking, pizza on steroids.

Should I eat it? Probably not. But will I eat it? You bet! Imagine the best ciabatta you ever had, toasted to a flaky, buttery, full, and complete crispy shatter. Imagine it as a grilled cheese sandwich, oozing with gooey, tangy cheese, with a crisp cracker-like cheesy outer edge, referred to as the frico, and just the right garnish on top to maximize its rewarding fullness. Yes, this is the ultimate grilled cheese in a pan. Crunchy, gooey, tangy, buttery, comforting—what's not to like?

WHAT THE FREAK IS A FRICO?

Properly defined, a frico is a classic dish associated with the Friulia region in the northeastern corner of Italy that is made of baked or fried shredded potatoes and cheese that crisps up in between the potatoes (kind of like a potato latke with crispy cheese bits). In the context of this book, one of the distinguishing characteristics of Detroit-style deep-pan pizza is the melting of cheese over the side of the crust and down along the outer edge, between the dough and the pan. As the cheese bakes, it crisps up into a

cracker-like wafer, darker than the crust itself, with a wonderful crispy texture and intense cheese flavor. So we are borrowing the term frico to describe this characteristic. However, instead of crispy potatoes, our frico is a bonus cheese crust that adds yet one more layer of flavor and complexity to an already amazing pizza.

I call this style deep-pan pizza rather than deep-dish pizza for a couple of reasons. The first is that I want to distinguish it from Chicago-style deep dish, which is a worthy category unto itself, a casserole pie in the style of its Italian antecedent, pizza rustica. However, deep-pan pizza, known in some circles as "square pizza" (even when not baked in square pans) and also called deep-dish or simply pan pizza by some pizza chains, has its own distinctive characteristics. Regardless of the various names, though, when I have a properly made deep-pan pizza, I wonder why it hadn't become the rage even sooner? When done right, this style has everything we desire in a pizza as well as, perhaps, the one thing we don't tend to want: lots of crust. On the other hand, and again only when it has been properly prepared, it is easy to ignore the abundance of dough because, frankly, the crust is just so freaking good.

Names can be very confusing. Is deep-pan pizza the same as Detroit-style pizza? Not to muddy the waters, the answer is yes and no. Detroit-style is definitely deep-pan pizza (and so is Chicago-style deep-dish pizza, but that's not what we're making here). The term Detroit-style is really more of a marketing term, not one

---

Richly caramelized undercrust and *frico*—like the best toast you ever had!

you'll hear in Detroit, where this is just called pizza. But because the method is so closely associated with Detroit and with Buddy's, Jet's, and the other great pizzerias of that city (where this style originated), the term makes it easier to identify this pizza when it shows up in other cities. Don't be surprised to find Detroit-style deep-pan pizza in cities like Brooklyn, Washington, DC, and even Telluride, Colorado, and Frisco, Texas, where it often veers off into creative versions never seen in Detroit and is sometimes simply called square pizza. Deep-pan pizza is also made by the big chains, like Dominoes and Pizza Hut, where it is often just called pan pizza. So, to avoid confusing our version of Detroit-inspired deep-pan pizza with all the other versions out there, I will refer to it throughout this book as deep-pan pizza and let Detroit bask in its reflected glory.

How did I miss knowing about this product during my research trips for *American Pie: My Search for the Perfect Pizza*? It just wasn't on my radar then, almost as if the folks from Detroit wanted to keep it under wraps to prevent the mainstream food world from hijacking and bastardizing it (which, as we can all see, is what is happening now, so perhaps they had a point). Or, maybe, even after the nearly eighty years since its "invention," it is simply an idea whose time has finally come, like the resurgence of Detroit itself.

If this pizza had been invented in Naples, there would probably be a DOC-like organization surrounding it, codifying the rules required to allow you to call your pizza Detroit-style or deep-pan pizza. Who knows? It might still happen, as deep-pan devotees begin to identify its rubrics and market it with "official" Detroit-style rules the way the Vera Pizza Napoletana folks in Naples did. However, until the day that arrives, we will adhere to the only rule that really matters in the end: the flavor rule (i.e., flavor rules!). For that reason, I have not required that you buy the blue steel rectangular pans that Buddy's and the other famous Detroit pizzerias use (see page 6); I ask only that you follow the given commonsense steps, which will enable you to make a pizza every bit as good as theirs in whatever size and shape baking pans you have on hand. Must you use Wisconsin brick cheese as they do? No. In fact many pizzerias don't (because it's pricey and hard to find), and many alternative options are provided and even encouraged, though it's hard to beat that wonderfully tangy, buttery Wisconsin brick cheese if you can find it (see page 9).

So, in this chapter, I am going to share with you a method that will enable you to use your home oven to make a deep-pan pizza—whether you call it Detroit-style, or deep-dish, or square—that is every bit as good as and maybe even better than one you can buy in Detroit or anywhere else in the country where this style is popping up like dandelions in spring. You don't need a wood-fired oven or any fancy tools. You just need a

2- or 3-inch-deep square or rectangular (or circular) cake pan and the ingredients listed, and I promise that you will fall completely under its thrall. The following recipes include enough topping ingredients for two 9 by 9-inch pizzas. However, since you may be using either larger or smaller pans, use the chart on page 15 to determine how much dough and cheese you will need and adjust the amount of other ingredients accordingly.

BEFORE YOU GET STARTED

You will discover, as you explore the various topping recipes and recommendations, how many of these pizzas have been inspired by other dishes, especially popular sandwiches. You already know that one of my favorite definitions for pizza is "dough with something on it" and that a sandwich is basically "dough with something in it." That's about as close a kissing cousin to pizza as it gets. Whenever I need inspiration for a new pizza, I nearly always begin my creative process by thinking about my favorite sandwiches, and then I try to figure out how to translate that into a pizza format. You will see this approach at work in a number of the pizzas that follow, though I have also tapped into other iconic dishes, like spaghetti and meatballs, for similar inspiration. My hope is that you will soon tap into your own food and taste memories and start adapting those recipes into memorable deep-pan pizzas of your own creation.

WHAT IS THE BEST WAY TO ADD ANCHOVIES TO A PIZZA?

Some people love them and some never will. For those who do, these salty, intensely flavored fillets can be added to almost any kind of pizza by following this one rule: never put them on the top of the pizza, where they will dry out while baking, almost turning into anchovy jerky. Instead, lay them under the cheese. For deep-pan pizzas, the best time to add them is right after the final dimpling and just before the first layer of cheese (that is, prior to the final 4-hour pan rise), so that they can be enveloped by both the cheese and the rising dough. This protects the anchovies from the intense oven heat and allows them to soften almost to the point of turning into what can only be described as anchovy butter. You might even be able to convert a few anchovy-averse people to the other side if you use this method.

THE CLASSIC RED STRIPE

MAKES TWO 9 BY 9-INCH PIZZAS

This pizza is probably the one you should start with, just to perfect your system and determine how your oven and baking shelf best need to be set. Once you've nailed it all down, you can make all of the other deep-pan pizzas that follow or even create your own variations. Then again, once you've made this one you may never need or want to make any other version, as the red stripe is about as close to heaven on earth as a pizza can take you. Start out with the classic White Flour Dough (page 27) before branching into country-style and sourdough, at least until you establish your benchmarks.

If you are considering adding a topping, you should know that many fans of this pizza also like to top it with pepperoni, which is the most iconic Detroit topping. If you are among those fans, feel free to add enough slices, where indicated in the instructions (just prior to the final addition of cheese), to cover the surface. Also, make sure you take the sauce out of the refrigerator about 2 hours before you are ready to bake.

Any Master Dough (pages 27–35)	1 pound brick, mozzarella, fontina, Muenster, or provolone cheese (or combination), cut into ¼-inch cubes (see page 9)	1 cup sliced pepperoni (optional) 1 cup Crushed Tomato Pizza Sauce (page 46) or All-Purpose Marinara Pizza Sauce (page 49)

Five hours before baking the pizzas, begin panning and dimpling the dough, at 20-minute intervals, as shown on page 13. After three to four rounds of dimpling and resting over the course of an hour, the dough will have relaxed enough to cover the whole pan. At this point, top the dough with half of the cheese cubes and gently press them into the dough (see page 15). Then allow 4 hours for the final rise. The dough will bubble up around the cheese and rise significantly in the pan.

Twenty minutes before assembling and baking the pizza, preheat the oven to 500°F (450°F for convection). Just before baking, top the dough with a layer of pepperoni slices (if using) and then the remaining half of the cheese cubes, making sure to get plenty around the edges, where the dough meets the pan.

CONTINUED >

Bake the pizza on the middle shelf of the oven for 8 minutes. Then rotate the pan 180 degrees and continue to bake 7 to 9 minutes longer, or until the cheese caramelizes to a golden brown and the pepperoni bubbles and browns. The undercrust of the dough should also caramelize to a rich golden brown, and the outer edge of the pizza should form a dark brown, thin, crispy cheese crust—the frico.

Transfer the baked pizza to the stovetop or to a heatproof counter. Using an offset spatula or bench blade, carefully slide it around the edge, between the crust and the side of the pan, and then lift the pizza out of the pan and slide it onto a cutting board. Use a spoon or squirt bottle to drizzle two or three stripes (or a crosshatch) of pizza sauce across the top, then cut into 3- or 4-inch squares and serve.

NAILING THE BAKE

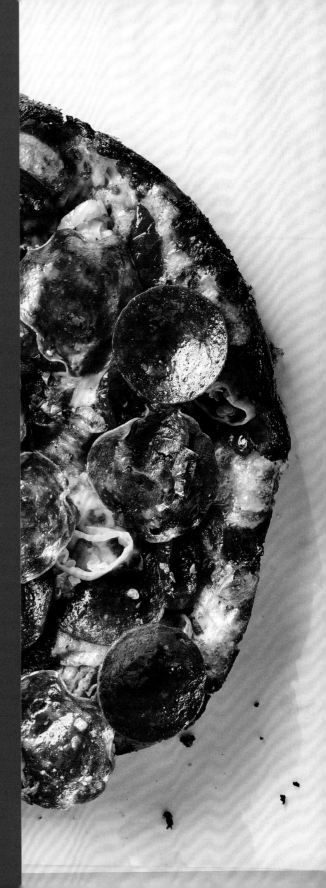

You may have to experiment with the placement of your oven shelf and baking time, depending on how your oven bakes. The key is to have the undercrust turn crisp and golden at the same time that the cheese on top bubbles and caramelizes. You can use a metal icing or offset spatula to lift one of the corners to check for caramelization. You may have to experiment with shelf placement and baking time, depending on how your oven bakes.

If the undercrust seems done before the cheese caramelizes, you can finish off the top of the pizza by turning on the broiler, but watch it carefully, because the pizza will brown within a minute or two. Conversely, if the top of your pizza or focaccia appears done (golden brown) but the undercrust is still cream colored and not caramelized or golden brown, there are steps you can take to solve the problem. At times like this, aluminum foil can be your best friend. You can buy a number of additional baking minutes by loosely covering the top of the pizza with foil (loosely, so that it doesn't trap steam) and also lowering the pan to the next shelf down in order to get it closer to the heat source. Every oven is different, so it may take a few attempts before you find the temperature setting and baking-shelf sweet spot.

BACON AND EGG

Bacon-and-egg pizzas are no longer viewed as an exotic concept, though it seemed they were so avant garde just a few short years ago. In fact, I think the concept is such an obvious pizza winner that it's no longer a matter of "wait, what?" but one of learning how to execute it to perfection. Some of the more adventurous pizzerias, instead of making it with bacon, use cubes of guanciale, a wonderful cured and spiced pork jowl delicacy that cooks to such fatty crispness as to induce rapturous tears. So I have no problem if you want to swap that in here (or you can also use cubes of pancetta, which is essentially bacon without the smoke). However, bacon is never shabby, so the following version makes a perfect BETA pizza (bacon, egg, tomato, and arugula). We'll revisit guanciale in another pizza on page 146.

Now for some math. The number of eggs per pizza will be determined by the size of the pan and personal taste. Small personal pizzas (6 by 6 inches) need only 1 egg, while some pans (9 by 9 inches) can handle up to two, or even 4 eggs for large rectangular pans, one in each quadrant.

Any Master Dough (pages 27–35)

1 pound slab bacon, cut into ½-inch cubes, or thick-cut sliced bacon, cut into ½-inch batons

1 pound brick, Muenster, or mozzarella-Cheddar blend, cut into ¼-inch cubes (see page 9)

6 Roma tomatoes, cut into ½-inch cubes

2 cups baby arugula

2 tablespoons olive oil

2 tablespoons balsamic vinegar

4 large eggs

Salt and freshly ground pepper

Five hours before baking the pizza, begin panning and dimpling the dough, at 20-minute intervals, as shown on page 13. After three to four rounds of dimpling and resting, the dough will have relaxed enough to cover the whole pan. At this point, top the dough with half of the cheese cubes and press them into the dough (see page 15). Then allow 4 hours for the final rise. The dough will bubble up around the cheese and rise significantly in the pan.

CONTINUED >

While the dough is rising, cook the bacon cubes in a large frying pan over medium-high heat, stirring until the pieces begin to render their fat and just begin browning. If using sliced bacon, bake it at 375°F (350°F for convection) on a sheet pan until lightly browned and crisp. Immediately remove the bacon from the heat and set it aside to cool.

While the dough is still rising, combine the cubed tomatoes, arugula, oil, and balsamic vinegar in a large bowl. Gently toss until everything is evenly coated with the oil and vinegar, and season with salt and pepper. Refrigerate until ready to assemble the pizzas.

Twenty minutes before assembling and baking the pizza, preheat the oven to 500°F (450°F for convection). Remove a small amount of the dressed arugula/tomato mixture from the bowl (about ½ cup for a large pizza or ¼ cup for a small one) and set it aside to use as garnish. Spread the remaining tomato and arugula mixture over the dough. Top with the bacon cubes and the remaining half of the cheese cubes, making sure to get plenty around the edges, where the dough meets the pan.

Bake on the middle shelf of the oven for 8 minutes. While the pizza is baking, crack the eggs into individual bowls. Remove the pan from the oven and add 1 or 2 eggs, one in each quadrant, on a large pie; if you are baking small pies, add 2 eggs on top of each. Return the pan to the oven, rotate it 180 degrees, and bake 7 to 9 minutes longer, or until the bacon cubes are crisp and golden, the cheese is fully melted, the egg whites are set but the yolks are still runny, and the dough is springy to the touch.

Transfer the baked pizza to the stovetop or to a heatproof counter. Using an offset spatula or bench blade, carefully slide it around the edge, between the crust and the side of the pan, and then lift the pizza out of the pan and slide it onto a cutting board. Garnish with the remaining arugula mixture and let it wilt on the hot pizza for about 60 seconds. Then cut into 3- or 4-inch squares and serve.

PEPPERONI DELUXE

In the realm of Detroit-style deep-pan pizza, pepperoni pizza is king. And while Italians scoff at how pepperoni doesn't even exist in Italy, where superior forms of salumi rule, Americans don't seem to care one bit. Although I truly love authentic Genoan and spicy Calabrian salumi, I think the person who turned those originals into the paprika-dominated hybrid that we call pepperoni was on to something. In fact, I've had artisanal pepperoni that makes me proud to be an American, because it delivers amazing flavor that equals that of the Italian imports. There are, of course, okay brands and better brands, but for this pizza the key is to use pepperoni with a diameter of 1 to 1½ inches, so that it cups up and crisps when baked, its oil (okay, grease) trapped in the curled cup. You can always make a simple pepperoni pizza with just sauce, cheese, and pepperoni, but this deluxe version pushes the envelope and adds the bright acidity of pickled peppers to boost the flavor experience. After trying this version, I fear you may be ruined forever when it comes to pepperoni pizzas.

Any Master Dough (pages 27–35)

1 pound brick, Muenster, mozzarella, provolone, or Cheddar cheese (or a combination), cut into ¼-inch cubes (see page 9)

1 cup Crushed Tomato Pizza Sauce (page 46) or All-Purpose Marinara Pizza Sauce (page 49)

4 ounces pepperoni, thinly sliced

½ cup pepperoncini or pickled Peppadew-style peppers, sliced crosswise, with brine

½ cup Secret Sauce or hoagie spread, plus more as needed (pages 59–60; optional)

Five hours before baking the pizza, begin panning and dimpling the dough, at 20-minute intervals, as shown on page 13. After three to four rounds of dimpling and resting, the dough will have relaxed enough to cover the whole pan. At this point, top the dough with half of the cheese cubes and press them into the dough (see page 15). Then allow 4 hours for the final rise. The dough will bubble up around the cheese and rise significantly in the pan.

CONTINUED >

Twenty minutes before assembling and baking the pizza, preheat the oven to 500°F (450°F for convection). Spread a thin coat of pizza sauce over the dough and cover the sauce with half of the pepperoni slices. Top with the remaining half of the cheese cubes, making sure to get plenty around the edges, where the dough meets the pan. Sprinkle the peppers over the cheese, then add another layer of pepperoni.

Bake on the middle shelf of the oven for 8 minutes. Then rotate the pan 180 degrees and continue baking 7 to 9 minutes longer, until the cheese is bubbly and the dough is springy to the touch.

Transfer the baked pizza to the stovetop or to a heatproof counter. Using an offset spatula or bench blade, carefully slide it around the edge, between the crust and the sides of the pan, and then lift the pizza out of the pan and slide it onto a cutting board. Dot the top of the pizzas with Secret Sauce or hoagie spread, if using. Let set for at least 1 minute, then cut into 3- or 4-inch squares. Serve with additional Secret Sauce or hoagie spread on the side, if desired.

KUNDALINI CAULIFLOWER

My first job after college, way back in 1971, was in Boston at an organic vegetarian restaurant called Root One Café, where I fell in love with cooking and created my first menu item: a garlicky baked cauliflower casserole that I called Kundalini Cauliflower. This was way before the current cauliflower craze, but nevertheless it became a very popular dish, one that I still make from time to time as a side dish and now have adapted for pizza, where it's a perfect flavor option. It's easy to make, super delicious, and still tastes as original as it did in 1971!

Any Master Dough (pages 27–35)

1 pound fontina, brick, Muenster, Cheddar, or provolone cheese (or a combination), cut into ¼-inch cubes (see page 9)

1 small head cauliflower, separated into florets

¼ cup red wine vinegar

1 cup olive oil

2 tablespoons freshly squeezed lemon juice

1 tablespoon Dijon mustard

8 garlic cloves, peeled and coarsely chopped

½ teaspoon kosher salt, plus more as needed

⅛ teaspoon freshly ground black pepper, plus more as needed

4 Roma tomatoes, cut into ½-inch cubes

¼ cup coarsely chopped flat-leaf parsley, for garnish

Five hours before baking the pizza, begin panning and dimpling the dough, at 20-minute intervals, as shown on page 13. After three to four rounds of dimpling, the dough will have relaxed enough to cover the whole pan. At this point, top the dough with half of the cheese cubes and press them into the dough (see page 15). Then allow 4 hours for the final rise. The dough will bubble up around the cheese and rise significantly in the pan.

While the dough is rising, wash and dry the cauliflower florets, then cut them into ½-inch pieces and put them in a bowl. In a blender, combine the vinegar, oil, lemon juice, mustard, chopped garlic, salt, and pepper and puree for about 20 seconds (or whisk the ingredients in a bowl) to make a smooth dressing. Taste and add more salt and pepper, if needed. Pour the dressing over the cauliflower pieces and toss until evenly coated. Refrigerate until you are ready to assemble the pizzas. (This mixture can be prepared in advance and held for up to 2 or 3 days.)

Twenty minutes before assembling and baking the pizza, preheat the oven to 500°F (450°F for convection). Top the dough with the remaining half of the cheese cubes, concentrating on the outer edge of the dough. Using a slotted spoon to allow excess dressing to drain back into the bowl, spoon an even layer of the cauliflower mixture over the dough. Top with the tomato pieces and drizzle 1 to 2 tablespoons of the remaining cauliflower dressing over the tomatoes.

Bake on the middle shelf of the oven for 8 minutes. Then rotate the pan 180 degrees and continue baking 7 to 9 minutes longer, until the cauliflower and tomatoes begin to char, the cheese is bubbly, and the dough is springy to the touch.

Transfer the baked pizza to the stovetop or to a heatproof counter. Using an offset spatula or bench blade, carefully slide it around the edge, between the crust and the side of the pan, and then lift the pizza out of the pan and slide it onto a cutting board. Drizzle a tablespoon or two of any remaining marinade over the top. Garnish with the parsley, cut into 3- or 4-inch squares and serve.

PHILLY-STYLE ROAST PORK WITH BROCCOLI RABE

MAKES TWO 9 BY 9-INCH PIZZAS

Philly-style roast pork sandwiches are rapidly rising in the pantheon of legendary Philadelphia foods, which includes cheesesteaks, among several others, and now many fans claim that the roast pork sandwich has surpassed the cheesesteak as the city's premier sandwich. As an omnivore with little self-control when it comes to these classics, I can only say that I love both sandwiches equally, with a fervor that can sometimes be embarrassing. There is some controversy regarding roast pork sandwiches concerning the use of broccoli rabe, the slightly bitter leaf that resembles mustard greens and kale. For this pizza version, rabe is just one of the options. For those who want something less bitter, there is a spinach alternative. I have found that baby arugula and baby kale also work quite nicely. Provolone is the Philly cheese of choice, but some places offer either a mild or medium-aged provolone or simply some other form of mild cheese, like good old American processed cheese. As a lover of cheese, I always come down on the side of the sharper, more aged varieties.

For this pizza, rather than use thinly sliced pork, as they do on the sandwiches at most places, I've opted to use slowly braised roasted pork chunks that brown and crisp nicely without drying out when you bake them on top of the pizza. My goal is to let the spirit of a juicy roast pork sandwich shine through, while not adhering strictly to the letter of the law. This pizza may, quite possibly, be my favorite of them all. (Well, then again, there's the Philly Cheesesteak Pizza on page 112.)

The pork shoulder roast (aka Boston butt) will make more than any one pizza can hold (unless you can find a butcher who will sell you a smaller 2-pound portion), but the meat freezes well and can be used for a number of meals: it can be reheated with barbecue sauce and served with creamy coleslaw and corn bread, as we did at my restaurant, Brother Juniper's Café, back in the day.

The roast pork should be prepared at least 1 day ahead, so plan accordingly.

CONTINUED >

Any Master Dough
(pages 27–35)

1 pound brick, provolone
(mild or aged), fontina, or
Muenster cheese, cut into
¼-inch cubes (see page 9)

¼ cup olive oil

1 cup very thinly sliced
red bell pepper (from
1 large pepper)

1 cup very thinly sliced
yellow or white onions
(from 1 large onion)

6 garlic cloves,
finely chopped

½ teaspoon salt, plus
more as needed

⅛ teaspoon freshly
ground black pepper,
plus more as needed

6 cups boiling water with
1 teaspoon salt

3 cups broccoli rabe,
baby spinach, baby kale,
or baby arugula

2 cups Roast Pork
(page 84)

4 to 6 Roma tomatoes,
cut into ½-inch cubes
(about 2 cups; optional)

¼ cup Secret Sauce
(page 59–60) or hoagie
spread, for serving

Five hours before baking the pizza, begin panning and dimpling the dough, at 20-minute intervals, as shown on page 13. After three to four rounds of dimpling and resting, the dough will have relaxed enough to cover the whole pan. At this point, top the dough with half of the cheese cubes and press them into the dough (see page 15). Then allow 4 hours for the final rise. The dough will bubble up around the cheese and rise significantly in the pan.

While the dough is rising, heat the oil in a skillet over medium heat. When the oil is hot, add the peppers and onions and sauté, stirring occasionally, until they sweat, become shiny, and soften. Add the garlic and continue stirring for 1 minute longer. Stir in the salt and pepper, remove the pan from the heat, and set it aside to cool. Taste and add more salt and pepper, if desired.

Bring the salted water to a boil, drop in the broccoli rabe or other greens, and blanch in simmering water for 1 minute. While the broccoli rabe simmers, fill a bowl with cold water and ice. Drain the greens in a colander or strainer and then plunge them into the ice water to stop the cooking. Drain and set aside.

Twenty minutes before assembling and baking the pizza, preheat the oven to 500°F (450°F for convection). Top the pizza generously with chunks of the roast pork. Spread the onion-pepper mixture over the pork and top with the remaining half of the cheese cubes, making sure to get plenty around the edges, where the dough meets the pan.

Bake on the middle shelf of the oven for 8 minutes. Then rotate the pan 180 degrees and continue baking 7 to 9 minutes longer, or until the cheese is bubbly, the dough is springy to the touch, and the pork and peppers develop a crusty edge.

Remove the pan from the oven and use a pair of tongs or a fork to spread the blanched greens over the pizza. Top the greens with the diced tomato. Return the pan to the oven for 1 minute.

Transfer the baked pizza to the stovetop or to a heatproof counter. Using an offset spatula or bench blade, carefully slide it around the edge, between the crust and the sides of the pan, and then lift the pizza out of the pan and slide it onto a cutting board. Drizzle any remaining pork glaze over the top. Let set for at least 1 minute, then cut into 3- or 4-inch squares and serve with your choice of Secret Sauce or hoagie spread on the side.

CONTINUED >

ROAST PORK

MAKES ENOUGH FOR FOUR 9 X 9-INCH PIZZAS

One 3- to 4-pound
Boston butt

3 tablespoons olive oil,
plus more as needed

2 tablespoons granulated
garlic (not garlic salt)

1 teaspoon dried parsley

½ teaspoon kosher salt

¼ teaspoon dried thyme

¼ teaspoon mild paprika

¼ teaspoon freshly
ground black pepper

¼ teaspoon
ground rosemary

½ cup beef broth

½ cup red wine,
additional beef broth,
or apple cider

1 teaspoon fennel seeds

Preheat the oven to 350°F (conventional or convection). Brush the pork butt with some oil. Then mix together the garlic, dried parsley, salt, thyme, paprika, pepper, and rosemary in a small bowl and rub it over the whole surface of the pork.

In a Dutch oven or ceramic casserole with a lid, heat the oil over medium-high heat. When the oil is hot, sear the pork butt on all sides until browned and the spices form a slight crust, 60 to 90 seconds on every side. Add the broth, wine, and fennel seeds. Cover the pot and transfer to the preheated oven. Lower the temperature to 250°F (225°F for convection) and roast in the oven for 4 to 6 hours.

When the pork is fork tender, transfer it to a bowl or platter. Then strain the pan juice into a bowl, discard the solids, and set the juice aside with the pork to cool at room temperature for about 1 hour. When the pork has cooled, cut it into 1-inch chunks. Then refrigerate the meat and the juices in separate covered containers overnight or up to 5 days or freeze for about 1 hour, until you are ready to assemble the pizza.

After the fat in the juice separates and solidifies, collect and discard it; retain the pure jus. Warm the jus and drizzle it over the pizza when it comes out of the oven.

MUSHROOMS TO THE MAX

MAKES TWO 9 BY 9-INCH PIZZAS

As a child, I always felt that mushrooms on a pizza were an unfulfilled promise. There seemed to be something of greatness lurking within those earthy fungi, but for the most part, they were always just a sidekick to whatever else was on the pie. Then, in my early adult years, the world of wild mushrooms opened up, and a bit later I was introduced to the mysterious depths and complexities of truffles. Most of us are now aware of this option, and we expect a mushroom to deliver something beyond those bland "buttons" of yore. Now we want them to take us on a gastronomic journey. But mostly, I think, we like them with garlic and salt and lately, with a splash of truffle oil. Since most of us can't afford an actual truffle, the recipe suggests using truffle oil as a finishing garnish to boost the flavor of these tasty fungi to an even higher level. If you are fortunate enough to have access to actual black or white truffles, by all means shave thin slices over the top instead of using the oil. That would really take it to the max!

Any Master Dough (pages 27–35)

1 pound brick, fontina, Muenster, or Gruyère cheese (or a combination), cut into ¼-inch cubes (see page 9)

8 ounces fresh shiitake, cremini, morels, or other wild mushrooms (or a combination)

2 tablespoons olive oil

6 garlic cloves, finely chopped

¼ teaspoon kosher salt, plus more as needed

Freshly ground pepper

6 Roma or Campari tomatoes, cut into ¼-inch-thick slices, or 1 cup Crushed Tomato Pizza Sauce (page 46) or All-Purpose Marinara Pizza Sauce (page 49)

White truffle oil, for garnish

¼ cup coarsely chopped flat-leaf parsley

Five hours before baking the pizzas, begin panning and dimpling the dough, at 20-minute intervals, as shown on page 13. After three to four rounds of dimpling and resting, the dough will have relaxed enough to cover the whole pan. At this point, top the dough with half of the cheese cubes and press them into the dough (see page 15). Then allow 4 hours for the final rise. The dough will bubble up around the cheese and rise significantly in the pan.

CONTINUED >

While the dough is rising, stem the mushrooms, wipe off the caps with a wet paper towel, and slice the caps into ¼-inch-thick slices. (If the stems are young and soft, you can chop them up and add them to the caps; otherwise discard them or use in a stock.) Heat a large pan over medium-high heat. When the pan is hot, add the oil, the chopped garlic, and the mushrooms and stir until combined. Lower the heat to medium and continue stirring until the mushrooms begin to sweat and soften, becoming shiny and limp (you can accelerate this by covering the pan with a lid for a minute or two to steam the mushrooms). Remove the pan from the heat and season with salt and pepper, starting with ¼ teaspoon kosher salt and a couple of pinches of pepper, and adding more as needed. Set the mushrooms aside to cool.

Twenty minutes before assembling and baking the pizza, preheat the oven to 500°F (450°F for convection). Cover the pizza with a layer of sliced tomatoes or with a thin layer of pizza sauce. Then, using a slotted spoon, top with an even layer of mushrooms. If there is any juice left in the pan, reduce it over medium-high heat until it thickens, and set it aside. Top the pizza with the remaining half of the cheese cubes, making sure to get plenty around the edges, where the dough meets the pan.

Bake on the middle shelf for 8 minutes. Then rotate the pan 180 degrees and continue baking 7 to 9 minutes longer, until the cheese is bubbly, the mushrooms are slightly charred, and the dough is springy to the touch.

Transfer the baked pizza to the stovetop or to a heatproof counter. Using an offset spatula or bench blade, carefully slide it around the edge, between the crust and the sides of the pan, and then lift the pizza out of the pan and slide it onto a cutting board. Drizzle the reduced mushroom liquid, if there is any, over the mushrooms. Then drizzle with a small amount of the truffle oil. Garnish the top with the parsley. Let set for at least 1 minute, then cut into 3- or 4-inch squares and serve.

BEEF BRISKET WITH BURNT ENDS

MAKES TWO 9 BY 9-INCH PIZZAS

I made my first culinary pilgrimage to Kansas City back in 1984, and it was a life-changing event. It was after dining there at Arthur Bryant's Barbecue that I became a burnt-ends fanatic. It confirmed the passion for burnt ends that I'd had since childhood and had kept secret from my family because I didn't want anyone to think I was crazy for eating those charcoal bits. "I am not alone!" I shouted when I gathered my Arthur Bryant burnt ends into a pile. And that, in short, is the genesis of this pizza. You don't need smoked meat or barbecue to make it, because it's actually about those crackly, crusty, charred morsels (along with the moist meat beneath it), and everything else is just an excuse to deliver them in an exciting way. Of course, if you have access to smoked brisket, it would not be a sin to use it here.

Unless you make a lot of pizzas, you will have a fair amount of leftover brisket. You can refrigerate it for up to 1 week, or freeze it for up to 3 months. For a delicious main course, reheat it with your favorite barbecue sauce and serve with coleslaw and corn bread, or just keep cranking out more of these pizzas whenever the urge hits.

Any Master Dough (pages 27–35)	1 medium onion, very thinly sliced	¼ cup pan jus from brisket
1 pound brick, mozzarella, Muenster, provolone, or Gruyère cheese (or a combination), cut into ¼-inch cubes (see page 9)	1 pound Roast Brisket (recipe follows)	Barbecue sauce (optional)
	4 to 6 Roma or Campari tomatoes, cut into ½-inch cubes	¼ cup chopped flat-leaf parsley
2 tablespoons olive or vegetable oil		

Five hours before baking the pizzas, begin panning and dimpling the dough, at 20-minute intervals, as shown on page 13. After three to four rounds of dimpling and resting, the dough will have relaxed enough to cover the whole pan. At this point, top the dough with half of the cheese cubes and press them into the dough (see page 15). Then allow 4 hours for the final rise. The dough will bubble up around the cheese and rise significantly in the pan.

While the dough is rising, heat the oil in a skillet over medium-low heat and lightly sauté the onions, just until they sweat and soften, about 10 minutes. Set aside to cool. Cut the cooled brisket into 1-inch-thick chunks.

Twenty minutes before assembling and baking the pizza, preheat the oven to 500°F (450°F for convection). Spoon the sautéed onions over the dough and top with chunks of brisket, evenly spaced (use as much as you'd like, but you do not have to use all the meat). Top the pizza with the remaining half of the cheese cubes, making sure to get plenty around the edges, where the dough meets the pan.

Bake on the middle shelf of the oven for 8 minutes, then rotate the pan 180 degrees and continue baking 7 to 9 minutes longer, until the cheese is bubbly and the onions and meat are browned, with some charred (yes, burnt!) edges.

While the pizza is baking, warm the jus in a saucepan over low heat.

Transfer the baked pizza to the stovetop or to a heatproof counter. Using an offset spatula or bench blade, carefully slide it around the edge, between the crust and the pan, and then lift the pizzas out of the pan and slide it onto a cutting board. Top the pizza with the tomato cubes and drizzle with a small amount of the jus. Drizzle with barbecue sauce (if using), and garnish with the chopped parsley. Let set for at least 1 minute, then cut into 3- or 4-inch squares and serve.

ROAST BRISKET
MAKES ENOUGH FOR FOUR 9 X 9-INCH PIZZAS

1 package dried onion soup mix (about 2 ounces)	2 tablespoons granulated garlic	12 ounces beef broth, cola, root beer, or ginger ale
	4 to 5 pounds beef brisket	

Preheat the oven to 275°F (250°F for convection). In a small bowl, combine the dry onion soup mix with the granulated garlic. Place the brisket in a Dutch oven or other covered baking dish (or slow cooker). Pour the dry mix over the brisket and roll the meat in the mixture to coat it on all sides. Lift the meat slightly and add the broth to the roasting pan. Cover the pan and place it in the oven. Roast for 5 to 7 hours or until the meat is fork tender.

Transfer the brisket to a platter to cool and let the juices cool in the pan for about 2 hours. Then cover the meat and the juices separately and refrigerate both. When the fat separates from the juices and hardens, scrape it off and discard, reserving the jus. The brisket will keep in the refrigerator for up to 1 week, or in the freezer for up to 3 months.

BANH MI

In Charlotte, North Carolina, where I now live, the benchmark for banh mi has been established by Mr. Le at Le's Sandwiches Café, where he demonstrates the secret of why banh mi is such a rising superstar in the sandwich pantheon: the proper balance of acid, crunch, and umami. Aside from having the right kind of loaf (crisp like a baguette but also softer and sweeter from the added presence of rice flour), the real stars of a banh mi sandwich (whose name translates as "bread") are the pickled vegetables. Of course, there are a few other Vietnamese tweaks that provide further differentiation, so with that in mind, here's a great way to deliver the essence of banh mi in the form of a pizza, where the crust is an ideal substitute for the roll.

Any Master Dough
(pages 27–35)

1 pound brick, mozzarella,
Muenster, provolone,
or fontina cheese (or a
combination), cut into
¼-inch cubes (see page 9)

2 tablespoons olive or
vegetable oil

6 garlic cloves, finely
chopped or pressed

1 cup chopped scallions

8 ounces ground pork
or ground chicken

2 tablespoons
Vietnamese fish sauce

2 tablespoons
Vietnamese or Thai
chile-garlic sauce
(such as Sriracha)

Zest of 1 lemon or lime

¼ teaspoon salt

⅛ teaspoon freshly
ground black pepper

4 tablespoons freshly
squeezed lemon or
lime juice

4 Roma or Capri
tomatoes, cut into ½-inch
cubes (optional)

½ cup Pickled Vegetables
(page 93)

2 jalapeño peppers,
seeded and cut
crosswise into thin
rounds (optional)

¾ cup mayonnaise

10 basil leaves, julienned

6 to 8 mint leaves,
coarsely chopped

¼ cup coarsely
chopped cilantro

CONTINUED >

Five hours before baking the pizza, begin panning and dimpling the dough, at 20-minute intervals, as shown on page 13. After three to four rounds of dimpling and resting, the dough will have relaxed enough to cover the whole pan. At this point, top the dough with half of the cheese cubes and press them into the dough (see page 15). Then allow 4 hours for the final rise. The dough will bubble up around the cheese and rise significantly in the pan.

While the dough is rising, heat the oil in a skillet over medium-high heat and lightly sauté the garlic and ½ cup of the scallions just until the scallions shine and turn bright green. Add the ground pork and cook, stirring, until the meat is cooked through. Add 1 tablespoon of the fish sauce, 1 tablespoon of the chile-garlic sauce, and the lemon zest and mix until combined. Stir in the salt and pepper. Using a slotted spoon, transfer the mixture to a bowl, leaving the juices in the pan, and bring the juice to a boil over high heat. Then lower the heat and simmer for about 1 minute until the juice has reduced and thickened. Remove the pan from the heat. When the juice has cooled, pour it back over the meat mixture and set the mixture aside to cool (if made more than 3 hours in advance, cover and refrigerate until needed).

In a small bowl, whisk together the mayonnaise, the remaining tablespoon of fish sauce, the remaining tablespoon of chile-garlic sauce, and the lemon juice. Cover and refrigerate until needed.

Twenty minutes before assembling and baking the pizza, preheat the oven to 500°F (450°F for convection). Top the dough with the remaining half of the cheese cubes, concentrating on the outer edge. Spoon the pork or chicken mixture over the cheese and sprinkle with the remaining ½ cup of the scallions.

Bake on the middle shelf of the oven for 8 minutes. Then rotate the pan 180 degrees and continue baking 7 to 9 minutes longer, until the cheese is bubbly and the meat is browned, with some charred edges.

Transfer the baked pizza to the stovetop or to a heatproof counter. Using an offset spatula or bench blade, carefully slide it around the edge, between the crust and the side of the pan, and then lift the pizza out of the pan and slide it onto a cutting board. Spoon the tomato cubes and pickled vegetables (a little goes a long way) over the pizza and top with the jalapeños. Drizzle the mayonnaise mixture over the toppings and garnish with the basil, mint, and cilantro. Let set for at least 1 minute, then cut into 3- or 4-inch squares and serve.

PICKLED VEGETABLES

MAKES APPROXIMATELY 2 CUPS

1 medium carrot, peeled	½ cup green or red cabbage, shredded	1½ tablespoons sugar
1 daikon radish, peeled		¼ teaspoon kosher salt
1 small cucumber	1½ tablespoons rice wine vinegar	⅛ teaspoon freshly ground black pepper

Using the large holes of a box grater (or a food processor fitted with the shredding disk), shred the carrot and daikon into thin strips. Peel and cut the cucumber crosswise into ¼-inch-thick disks, then cut each disk into 4 wedges.

Combine all of the vegetables in a mixing bowl and toss. Add 1 tablespoon of the vinegar, 1 tablespoon of the sugar, the salt, and pepper and toss to combine. Taste and adjust the seasoning by adding the remaining ½ tablespoon vinegar or sugar, if desired. Cover and refrigerate for up to 2 weeks.

VEGGIE "PEPPERONI"

MAKES TWO 9 BY 9-INCH PIZZAS

Now we're treading on some tricky soil. As I mentioned on page 75, pepperoni is really just a hack of traditional spicy Calabrese Italian salumi that is pretty much sneered at by Italophiles, a fact that has not affected its popularity on this side of the ocean. As a variation on this theme, my friend Brad English, who is also one of my partners in the website PizzaQuest.com, has come up with a unique hack of his own. Every month, he posts a new recipe or pizza idea based on a wild hunch or creative spark, and most of the time he hits it out of the ballpark. Somehow, he got the notion that broccoli stalks, once peeled and sliced into discs, could be rolled in spices, seasoned to taste, and look like pepperoni. Darn if it didn't work! I've adapted it here to be used on a deep-pan pizza, not only for vegetarians but also for anyone who likes the spicy flavor of pepperoni but not so much the grease. Yes, it's hard to think of pepperoni sans its grease, which seems so essential to its appeal, but maybe not anymore, as this playful, healthier variation demonstrates.

Any Master Dough (pages 27–35)

1 pound brick, mozzarella, Muenster, provolone, or fontina cheese (or a combination), cut into ¼-inch cubes (see page 9)

VEGGIE "PEPPERONI"

1½ teaspoons sweet paprika

1½ teaspoons granulated garlic powder

1 teaspoon ground fennel seeds

1 teaspoon ground mustard seeds

1 teaspoon ground red pepper flakes (optional)

½ teaspoon kosher salt

⅛ teaspoon cayenne pepper (optional)

⅛ teaspoon freshly ground black pepper

4 to 5 large broccoli stalks

1 tablespoon olive oil

1 tablespoon soy sauce

1½ teaspoons rice wine vinegar or red wine vinegar

1 cup Crushed Tomato Pizza Sauce (page 46) or All-Purpose Marinara Pizza Sauce (page 49)

6 Roma or Campari tomatoes, cut into ½-inch cubes (about 2 cups)

¼ cup chopped flat-leaf parsley

Five hours before baking the pizza, begin panning and dimpling the dough, at 20-minute intervals, as shown on page 13. After three to four rounds of dimpling and resting, the dough will have relaxed enough to cover the whole pan. At this point, spread half of the cheese cubes on top of the dough and press them into

CONTINUED >

the dough (see page 15). Then allow 4 hours for the final rise. The dough will bubble up around the cheese and rise significantly in the pan.

While the dough is rising, make the veggie "pepperoni." Preheat the oven to 350°F (325°F for convection). In a bowl, whisk together the paprika, garlic powder, fennel seeds, mustard seeds, red pepper flakes (if using), salt, cayenne pepper (if using), and black pepper until blended. Set aside.

Cut off the woody bottom of the broccoli stalks. If the stalks have a thick skin (most will), remove it with a vegetable peeler. If the stalks are young and thin skinned, there's no need to peel them. Cut the stalks crosswise into ⅛-inch-thick disks and add them to the bowl with the spice mixture. Then add the oil, soy sauce, and vinegar to the bowl and stir until the slices are evenly coated with the paste that has formed.

Line a sheet pan with parchment paper or a silicone baking mat and mist it lightly with vegetable spray oil. Spread the broccoli mixture evenly in the prepared pan and bake for approximately 8 minutes. Using a burger flipper, turn the pieces over and bake 6 to 8 minutes longer, or until the pieces begin to curl and slightly brown on the edges. Transfer the pan to a wire rack and let the broccoli cool.

Twenty minutes before assembling and baking the pizza, preheat the oven to 500°F (450°F for convection). Cover the dough with a thin layer of pizza sauce and spread half of the "pepperoni" over the sauce. Top the dough with the remaining half of the cheese cubes, making sure to get plenty around the edges, where the dough meets the pan. Sprinkle with the cubed tomatoes and then add another layer of "pepperoni."

Bake on the middle shelf of the oven for 8 minutes. Then rotate the pan 180 degrees and continue baking 7 to 9 minutes longer, or until the cheese is golden and bubbly and the dough is springy to the touch.

Transfer the baked pizza to the stovetop or to a heatproof counter. Using an offset spatula or bench blade, carefully slide it around the edge, between the crust and the side of the pan, and then lift the pizza out of the pan and slide it onto a cutting board. Garnish with the parsley. Let set for at least 1 minute, then cut into 3- or 4-inch squares and serve.

OLIVE AND ARTICHOKE MEDLEY

MAKES TWO 9 BY 9-INCH PIZZAS

This colorful topping combination is now offered in an increasing number of pizzerias. Marinated artichoke hearts are widely available in various sizes and in both jars and cans. Sometimes they are already quartered and sometimes not, so quarter them if needed. Usually, they come with their own tasty oil-and-vinegar marinade, so there's no need to reinvent the wheel. You can add the marinade to the other topping ingredients to expand the flavor of the whole medley. I like using both black and green olives because they each contribute their own flavor and visual contrast (you can even use the green ones stuffed with pimientos), but you can also use only one or the other if you prefer.

This colorful medley creates a beautiful and delicious vegetarian pizza. However, if you want to add meat, you can always add protein toppings to the artichoke-olive mixture just before baking. Pepperoni, crumbled bacon or sausage, cooked chicken, and shrimp are all popular add-ons, as are other deli meats, like salami and ham. The olive-and-artichoke medley is akin to a secret sauce: delicious by itself but even greater than the sum of its parts when combined with any other toppings you decide to include. You might want to keep a jar of the medley on hand to use as an extra topping for many of the other pizzas in this book.

Any Master Dough (pages 27–35)

1 pound brick, Muenster, mozzarella, fontina, or provolone cheese (or a combination), cut into ¼-inch cubes (see page 9)

6 marinated artichoke hearts, quartered, with marinade

½ cup sliced black olives

½ cup sliced green olives

½ cup diced red bell pepper

1 cup cherry tomatoes or grape tomatoes, halved

1 tablespoon olive oil

1 tablespoon lemon juice, or 1 teaspoon red wine vinegar

Salt and freshly ground pepper

¼ cup chopped flat-leaf parsley or basil, for garnish

¼ teaspoon dried oregano, for garnish

CONTINUED >

Five hours before baking the pizzas, begin panning and dimpling the dough, at 20-minute intervals, as shown on page 13. After three to four rounds of dimpling and resting, the dough will have relaxed enough to cover the whole pan. At this point, top the dough with half of the cheese cubes and press them into the dough (see page 15). Then allow 3 to 4 hours for the final rise. The dough will bubble up around the cheese and rise significantly in the pan.

While the dough is rising, combine the quartered artichoke hearts, along with any marinade in the jar or can (though no more than ½ cup), both types of olives, and the diced red bell pepper in a bowl. Gently fold in the tomatoes. Add the oil and lemon juice and gently toss until all the vegetables are evenly coated. Season with salt and pepper. Cover the bowl and refrigerate until you're ready to assemble the pizza.

Twenty minutes before assembling and baking the pizza, preheat the oven to 500°F (450°F for convection). Top the dough with the remaining half of the cheese cubes, making sure to get plenty around the edges, where the dough meets the pan. Spread 1½ cups of the artichoke-olive mixture over the cheese.

Bake on the middle shelf of the oven for 8 minutes. Then rotate the pan 180 degrees and continue to bake 7 to 9 minutes longer, or until the cheese caramelizes to a golden brown and the artichoke mixture bubbles and browns.

Transfer the baked pizza to the stovetop or to a heatproof counter. Using an offset spatula or bench blade, carefully slide it around the edge, between the crust and the side of the pan, and then lift the pizza out of the pan and slide it onto a cutting board. Garnish with the parsley and a sprinkle of dried oregano. Let set for 1 minute, then cut into 3- or 4-inch squares and serve.

LEMON, BROCCOLI, AND GARLIC

MAKES TWO 9 BY 9-INCH PIZZAS

Broccoli, like cauliflower, goes in and out of favor like the latest teenage pop star. But the fact is that both broccoli and cauliflower not only rate as highly as the tastiest of vegetables but also are among the most functional, especially with all those nooks and crannies that soak up flavor from, in this case, ample amounts of garlic and lemon. You might even say, after tasting this pizza, that broccoli is like the English muffin of vegetables, a veritable sponge of flavor absorption. The finishing touch here is the Lemon-Garlic Sauce, an easy-to-make aioli-like garnish that ties together all the flavors exactly the way a good sauce is supposed to. It weaves throughout the ingredients to connect and enhance the stars of the show—the broccoli florets—in much the same way a great supporting actor or actress in a film makes the film better. The Lemon-Garlic Sauce elevates a perfectly good dish into a memorable one.

Any Master Dough (pages 27–35)

1 pound brick, Muenster, provolone, mozzarella, fontina, or Cheddar cheese (or a combination), cut into ¼-inch-cubes (see page 9)

2 cups bite-size broccoli florets

4 garlic cloves, coarsely chopped

3 tablespoons olive oil

¼ cup freshly squeezed lemon juice

¼ teaspoon kosher salt, plus more as needed

⅛ teaspoon freshly ground black pepper, plus more as needed

4 Roma or Campari tomatoes, cut into ½-inch cubes

Lemon-Garlic Sauce (recipe follows), for drizzling

Five hours before baking the pizzas, begin panning and dimpling the dough, at 20-minute intervals, as shown on page 13. After three to four rounds of dimpling and resting, the dough will have relaxed enough to cover the whole pan. At this point, top the dough with half of the cheese cubes and press them into the dough (see page 15). Then allow 3 to 4 hours for the final rise. The dough will bubble up around the cheese and rise significantly in the pan.

Heat the oil in a skillet or wok over high heat. When the oil is hot, add the broccoli florets and the garlic, and sauté for approximately 3 minutes, or until the broccoli turns shiny and softens slightly. Add the lemon juice, salt, and pepper and stir until the florets are evenly coated. Immediately turn off the heat. Add more salt and pepper, if needed, and set the broccoli aside to cool.

Twenty minutes before assembling and baking the pizza, preheat the oven to 500°F (450°F for convection). Top the dough with the remaining half of the cheese cubes, making sure to get plenty around the edges, where the dough meets the pan. Spread the broccoli in an even layer over the cheese and top the broccoli with the tomato cubes. If there is any juice left in the sauté pan, drizzle it over the tomatoes and florets.

Bake on the middle shelf of the oven for 8 minutes. Then rotate the pan 180 degrees and continue baking 7 to 9 minutes longer, until the cheese is bubbly and the broccoli and tomatoes are slightly charred.

Transfer the baked pizza to the stovetop or to a heatproof counter. Using an offset spatula or bench blade, carefully slide it around the edge, between the crust and the side of the pan, and then lift the pizza out of the pan and slide it onto a cutting board. Drizzle with Lemon-Garlic Sauce. Let set for at least 1 minute, then cut into 3- or 4-inch squares and serve.

LEMON-GARLIC SAUCE
MAKES APPROXIMATELY 1 CUP

¾ cup mayonnaise

1 large garlic clove, finely minced or pressed

¼ cup freshly squeezed lemon juice

¼ cup freshly grated Parmesan, Romano, or Asiago cheese

In a bowl, combine the mayonnaise, garlic, and lemon juice and whisk until smooth. Stir in the cheese, cover, and refrigerate until needed. The sauce will keep in the refrigerator for up to 2 weeks.

THE SCLT (SMOKED CHICKEN, LETTUCE, AND TOMATOES)

MAKES TWO 9 BY 9-INCH PIZZAS

You can turn this SCLT into a BCLT (bacon and chicken instead of smoked chicken) or even into a simple BLT, but any way you make it, it will quickly become a family favorite. You can also replace the smoked chicken with smoked turkey, which may be easier to find at the deli. Any of these are really just variations on a classic theme, and as it is for sandwiches so it is for pizza: the secret is the sauce you drizzle over the top. In this case, it's a simple Thousand Island dressing variation that ties all the flavors together and makes them pop. You could also use ranch or any favorite creamy dressing, including blue cheese dressing, if you prefer; after all, it's your pizza. However, I think the sauce described here does all the heavy lifting with very little work on your part.

Any Master Dough (pages 27–35)

1 pound brick, provolone, Cheddar, Muenster, or Swiss cheese (or a combination), cut into ¼-inch cubes (see page 9)

½ cup mayonnaise

1 tablespoon ketchup

1 tablespoon red wine vinegar or apple cider vinegar

1 tablespoon dill pickle relish

1 tablespoon finely diced sweet onion

4 ounces sliced smoked chicken or turkey, cut into 2-inch matchsticks

4 ounces sliced smoked chicken or turkey, cut into 2-inch matchsticks

6 Roma or Campari tomatoes, cut into ½-inch cubes

2 cups chopped iceberg lettuce

1 sprig fresh dill, minced

Five hours before baking the pizza, begin panning and dimpling the dough, at 20-minute intervals as shown on page 13. After three to four rounds of dimpling and resting, the dough will have relaxed enough to cover the whole pan. At this point, top the dough with half of the cheese cubes and press them into the dough (see page 15). Then allow 4 hours for the final rise. The dough will bubble up around the cheese and rise in the pan.

While the dough is rising, in a bowl, whisk together the mayonnaise, ketchup, vinegar, relish, and onion and set aside or cover and refrigerate.

Twenty minutes before assembling and baking the pizza, preheat the oven to 500°F (450°F for convection). Cover the dough with the smoked chicken strips. Top with the remaining half of the cheese cubes, making sure to get plenty around the edges, where the dough meets the pan. Then top with the tomato cubes.

Bake on the middle shelf of the oven for 8 minutes. Then rotate the pan 180 degrees and continue baking 7 to 9 minutes longer, until the cheese is bubbly and golden and the dough is springy to the touch. While the pizza is baking, dress the lettuce with half of the mayonnaise dressing and toss until evenly coated.

Transfer the baked pizza to the stovetop or to a heatproof counter. Using an offset spatula or bench blade, carefully slide it around the edge, between the crust and the side of the pan, and then lift the pizza out of the pan and slide it onto a cutting board. Cover the top with the dressed lettuce, drizzle with the remaining half of the dressing, and garnish with the dill. Let set for at least 1 minute, then cut into 3- or 4-inch squares and serve.

REUBEN

As I have mentioned, many of my pizzas have been inspired by classic sandwiches and then modified and adapted to fit the deep-pan pizza model. Why not, since a sandwich fits my fundamental definition of a pizza ("dough with something on it or in it"). But the trick is putting it all together in a way that honors and even enhances the spirit and flavor of the original sandwich inspiration. I've seen Reuben pizzas on an increasing number of pizzeria menus, and there's a good reason for this. The Reuben is arguably one of the greatest sandwiches ever invented. It has everything you could want: toasty rye bread, melted gooey cheese (preferably Swiss), tangy sauerkraut (or coleslaw in some instances), and a creamy sauce that ties everything together with rich flavor and texture. It can be made with either corned beef or pastrami. In other words, it's a sandwich that does everything a pizza does, as you will find out when you try this version, which is ideally suited to the deep-pan style.

As a child who spent a lot of time eating in Jewish delis, I had another go-to sandwich beside the Reuben: corned beef, coleslaw, and Russian dressing on onion rye. The coleslaw and Russian dressing components made the whole sandwich sing. For that reason, I decided to include the coleslaw option here in lieu of sauerkraut. This coleslaw was the most popular side dish served at our restaurant, Brother Juniper's Café, many years ago.

Any Master Dough
(pages 27–35)

1 pound Swiss or Gruyére cheese, cut into ¼-inch cubes (see page 9)

8 ounces precooked pastrami or corned beef, thinly sliced

1¼ cups Reuben Sauce (page 107)

1½ cups Peter's Coleslaw (page 107)

4 to 6 Roma or Campari tomatoes, cut into ½-inch cubes (optional)

Five hours before baking the pizza, begin panning and dimpling the dough, at 20-minute intervals, as shown on page 13. After three to four rounds of dimpling and resting, the dough will have relaxed enough to cover the whole pan. At this point, top the dough with half of the cheese cubes and press them into the dough (see page 15). Then allow 4 hours for the final rise. The dough will bubble up around the cheese and rise significantly in the pan.

CONTINUED >

While the dough is rising, cut the pastrami or corned beef into ½-inch-wide, 1-inch-long strips. Place them in a bowl, cover, and refrigerate until you are ready to assemble the pizza. Make the Reuben Sauce, cover, and chill until the pizza leaves the oven. If using Peter's Coleslaw, make it at least 2 hours before assembling the pizza, cover, and chill until ready to use.

Twenty minutes before assembling and baking the pizza, preheat the oven to 500°F (450°F for convection). Cover the dough with the strips of pastrami or corned beef and top with the remaining half of the cheese cubes, making sure to get plenty around the edges, where the dough meets the pan.

Bake on the middle shelf of the oven for 8 minutes. Then rotate the pan 180 degrees and continue baking 7 to 9 minutes longer, until the cheese is bubbly and the meat develops some charred edges. Remove the pizza from the oven. If using sauerkraut, spread a layer over the pizza, top with the tomatoes (if using), and return the pan to the oven for 2 minutes to heat the kraut.

Transfer the baked pizza to the stovetop or to a heatproof counter. Using an offset spatula or bench blade, carefully slide it around the edge, between the crust and the side of the pan, and then lift the pizza out of the pan and slide it onto a cutting board. If using coleslaw instead of sauerkraut, spread a layer of the coleslaw over the pizza and drizzle with generous streaks of Reuben Sauce. Let set for at least 1 minute, then cut into 3- or 4-inch squares and serve.

REUBEN SAUCE
MAKES 1½ CUPS

¾ cup mayonnaise

¼ cup yogurt or
sour cream

¼ cup ketchup or
chile sauce

2 garlic cloves, pressed
or minced

1 teaspoon prepared
horseradish

2 tablespoons chopped
dill pickle or dill relish

2 tablespoons diced
sweet onion

¼ teaspoon
Worcestershire sauce

In a small bowl, whisk together the mayonnaise, yogurt, ketchup, garlic, horse-radish, dill pickle, onion, and Worcestershire sauce until blended. Cover and refrigerate for up to 2 weeks.

PETER'S COLESLAW
MAKES ABOUT 2½ CUPS

3 cups shredded or
finely chopped green
or red cabbage (from
about ¼ of a medium
cabbage)

3 tablespoons finely
diced sweet onion (such
as Vidalia, Walla Walla,
or Maui)

⅓ cup mayonnaise, plus
more as needed

1½ tablespoons sugar,
plus more as needed

2 teaspoons apple
cider vinegar, plus
more as needed

Pinch of freshly ground
black pepper

In a large bowl, toss the cabbage, onion, mayonnaise, sugar, vinegar, and pepper until well combined. Taste and adjust the seasoning by adding more sugar, vinegar, or mayo. Cover and keep chilled until ready to use. The coleslaw will keep in the refrigerator for up to 5 days.

SPAGHETTI AND MEATBALLS

It has become increasingly popular on restaurant menus to bring together two classic dishes, such as pizza with spaghetti and meatballs (or mac and cheese with pretty much anything), to create a delightful hybrid that is even better than the sum of its parts. To put it in perspective, how wonderful is buttery garlic bread served alongside spaghetti and meatballs? So why not swap out the garlic bread for a killer pizza crust and bring all the components together in one brilliant bite? I guarantee that your family, especially your kids, will thank you for this.

You can substitute an equal amount of ground chuck for the ground pork in the meatballs; or for a spicy and less labor-intensive alternative, try using Italian sausage instead of preparing meatballs from scratch.

Any Master Dough (pages 27–35)

1 pound brick, provolone, Muenster, mozzarella, or fontina cheese (or a combination), cut into ¼-inch cubes (see page 9)

16 Homemade Meatballs (page 111)

2 quarts water

1 teaspoon salt

8 ounces spaghetti, linguini, or rigatoni

2 tablespoons olive oil

1½ cups Crushed Tomato Pizza Sauce (pages 46) or All-Purpose Marinara Pizza Sauce (page 49)

½ cup freshly grated Parmesan, Romano, or Asiago cheese, plus more for serving (optional)

¼ cup chopped flat-leaf parsley

Five hours before baking the pizza, begin panning and dimpling the dough, at 20-minute intervals, as shown on page 13. After three to four rounds of dimpling and resting, the dough will have relaxed enough to cover the whole pan. At this point, top the dough with half of the cheese cubes and press them into the dough (see page 15). Then allow 4 hours for the final rise. The dough will bubble up around the cheese and rise in the pan.

While the dough is rising, cook the spaghetti. Bring 2 quarts of water to a boil, add the salt, and then add the pasta. Simmer, stirring, until the pasta is al dente (the

CONTINUED >

cooking time will vary, depending on the type and brand of pasta, so follow the instructions on the box). Drain thoroughly and transfer the cooked spaghetti to a large bowl. Add the oil, and stir until the pasta is evenly coated.

Heat the pizza sauce in a saucepan and bring to a mild simmer. Add the cooked meatballs to the sauce and simmer for about 5 minutes so that they can absorb some of the flavor from the sauce and impart some of their flavor to the sauce. Remove from the heat and reserve.

Twenty minutes before assembling and baking the pizzas, preheat the oven to 500°F (450°F for convection). Top the dough with the remaining half of the cheese cubes, making sure to get plenty around the edges, where the dough meets the pan. Use tongs or a slotted spoon to remove the meatballs from the sauce and transfer them to the pizza.

Pour the sauce over the cooked pasta in the bowl and stir until the pasta is evenly coated. Spread the pasta over the meatballs, leaving any remaining sauce in the bowl. Let some of the meatballs peek through the pasta.

Bake on the middle shelf of the oven for 8 minutes. Then rotate the pan 180 degrees and continue baking 7 to 9 minutes longer, until the cheese is bubbly, the meatballs are browned, and the pasta is slightly crisp. While the pizza is baking heat the remaining pasta sauce, if any, to just below a simmer.

Transfer the baked pizza to the stovetop or to a heatproof counter. Using an offset spatula or bench blade, carefully slide it around the edge, between the crust and the side of the pan, and then lift the pizza out of the pan and slide it onto a cutting board. Drizzle the pizza with any remaining sauce from the pasta bowl, then sprinkle with the Parmesan cheese (if using) and garnish with the parsley. Let set for at least 1 minute, then cut into 3- or 4-inch squares and serve. Feel free to add more grated cheese when serving.

HOMEMADE MEATBALLS

MAKES ABOUT 16 MEATBALLS

4 ounces ground beef chuck

4 ounces ground pork

1 egg

¼ cup dried breadcrumbs or Japanese panko

¼ cup milk

¼ cup freshly grated Parmesan, Romano, or Asiago cheese

¼ cup chopped flat-leaf parsley

¼ cup freshly grated mozzarella, provolone, or fontina cheese

⅛ teaspoon dried oregano (optional)

⅛ teaspoon dried thyme (optional)

4 garlic cloves, finely chopped or pressed (optional)

¼ teaspoon kosher salt

⅛ teaspoon freshly ground black pepper

In a bowl, mix together all of the ingredients with your hands or a large spoon.

Preheat the oven to 400°F (375°F for convection) and line a sheet pan with parchment paper or a silicone mat. Form the mixture into small balls, about the size of a cherry tomato or about 1 inch in diameter, and place them close together but not touching on the prepared sheet pan.

Bake on the middle shelf of the oven for 8 minutes. Then rotate the pan 180 degrees and bake 4 to 5 minutes longer, or until they start to brown on the underside and are springy to the touch.

Transfer the pan to a wire rack or trivet and let the meatballs cool at room temperature for 1 hour. If working far ahead, cover the pan of cooled meatballs with plastic wrap (or place them in a tightly sealed container) and refrigerate for up to 5 days. Unused meatballs can be stored in a freezer bag and frozen for up to 3 months.

PHILLY CHEESESTEAK

MAKES TWO 9 BY 9-INCH PIZZAS

No self-respecting Philly boy could resist including a cheesesteak pizza in a book like this. Cheesesteaks are such a huge part of Philadelphia's cultural identity that it's difficult to have an objective, rational conversation about them before emotions boil over and arguments ensue as to who makes the best one (sounds just like the pizza world, so the following pizza should really raise the volume). I've written extensively in *American Pie* about my favorite Philly cheesesteak, made at Mama's Pizzeria on Belmont Avenue in Bala Cynwyd, Pennsylvania. There are a number of reasons why I think Mama's is the best, not the least of which is that they use rib-eye steak instead of the typical top round, which is why I suggest rib eye in this recipe, though you can default to another (albeit lesser) cut if you prefer. They also use their house blend of three different cheeses instead of Velveeta or "cheese whiz" or the bland American cheese used by other places (don't get me started!). So, while the following is not an exact replica of the Mama's cheesesteak, it captures the spirit of that iconic sandwich and its inimitable flavors in a deep-pan pizza version. (Note: If you are using Cheddar, it should be no more than 25 percent of the total amount of cheese.)

You will also note that the instructions suggest finishing the pizza off with pizza sauce or with ketchup after it comes out of the oven. Why ketchup? This is one time when I think this much-maligned and often overused condiment is really appropriate, but that's just me. A cheesesteak is great with or without any sauce.

8 ounces rib eye or top round steak

½ teaspoon kosher salt, plus more as needed

¼ teaspoon freshly ground black pepper, plus more as needed

Any Master Dough (pages 27–35)

1 pound provolone, brick, mozzarella, fontina, Muenster, or white Cheddar cheese (or a combination), cut into ¼-inch cubes (see page 9)

¼ cup olive oil

2 cups yellow or white onions, cut into thin strips

8 garlic cloves, coarsely chopped (optional)

Secret Sauce (pages 59–60), for drizzling

½ cup Crushed Tomato Pizza Sauce (page 48), All-Purpose Marinara Pizza Sauce (page 49), or ketchup

Any time from 1 day ahead or up to 3 hours before baking the pizza, cut the steak into strips about 2 inches long and ¼ inch thick. If you prefer your steak rare, cut the strips ½ inch thick. Place the steak in a bowl, add salt and pepper and stir until evenly coated. Cover the bowl with plastic wrap and refrigerate until you're ready to assemble the pizza.

Five hours before baking the pizzas, begin panning and dimpling the dough, at 20-minute intervals, as shown on page 13. After three to four rounds of dimpling and resting, the dough will have relaxed enough to cover the whole pan. At that point, top the dough with half of the cheese cubes and press them into the dough (see page 15). Then allow 4 hours for the final rise. The dough will bubble up around the cheese and rise significantly in the pan.

While the dough is rising, heat the oil in a skillet over medium-high heat, add the onions, and sauté until they sweat, become shiny, and soften, about 5 minutes. Add the garlic and continue stirring for a minute or two longer to soften but only slightly brown the onions. Season with salt and pepper, then remove the pan from the heat and set aside to cool.

Twenty minutes before assembling and baking the pizza, preheat the oven to 500°F (450°F for convection). Top the dough with the remaining half of the cheese cubes, making sure to get plenty around the edges, where the dough meets the pan. Cover the cheese with the strips of meat, and spread the onion mixture over the meat. Drizzle a teaspoon or two of the Secret Sauce over the surface.

Bake on the middle shelf of the oven for 8 minutes. Then rotate the pan 180 degrees and continue baking 7 to 9 minutes longer, until the cheese is bubbly, the dough is springy to the touch, and the steak develops a crusty edge.

Transfer the baked pizza to the stovetop or to a heatproof counter. Using an offset spatula or bench blade, carefully slide it around the edge, between the crust and the side of the pan, and then lift the pizza out of the pan and slide it onto a cutting board. Season with salt and pepper and drizzle with the pizza sauce or ketchup. Let set for at least 1 minute, then cut into 3- or 4-inch squares and serve.

MOTOR CITY HAWAIIAN

MAKES TWO 9 BY 9-INCH PIZZAS

There is probably no pizza more polarizing than what is called Hawaiian pizza, and, ironically, it's not even Hawaiian. One version of its origin story claims that it was invented in 1962 by a Greek-Canadian, Sam Panopoulos, at the Satellite Restaurant in Chatham, Ontario. I guess this explains why so many versions are made with Canadian bacon. Sam said this pizza was inspired by his earlier experience preparing Chinese dishes, which commonly mix sweet and savory flavors. I find the sweet and savory flavor contrast can also be achieved with spicy ham, like capicola, as well as with bacon or pancetta. Regardless, it's the pineapple, with its Hawaiian association (and thus the name, even if not its true birthplace), that causes all the controversy. But I say that it's time for anyone who has a problem with pineapple (or any fruit) pizza topping to try this version and just get over it, because here's what happens when Detroit-style deep-pan pizza meets Hawaiian pineapple: pure magic!

Any Master Dough (pages 27–35)

1 pound brick, Muenster, mozzarella, fontina, Cheddar, or provolone cheese (or a combination), cut into ¼-inch cubes (see page 9)

4 ounces Canadian bacon, capicola ham, or cooked bacon, cut into ½-inch cubes

½ cup diced yellow or white onion

1 jalapeño pepper, seeded and diced (optional)

One 8-ounce can pineapple chunks or sliced pineapple, ½ fresh pineapple peeled and cut into ½-inch chunks or slices, or 6 ounces frozen pineapple pieces

½ cup Crushed Tomato Pizza Sauce (page 46) or All-Purpose Marinara Sauce (page 49; optional)

¼ cup chopped flat-leaf parsley

Five hours before baking the pizza, begin panning and dimpling the dough, at 20-minute intervals, as shown on page 13. After three to four rounds of dimpling and resting, the dough will have relaxed enough to cover the whole pan. At this point, top the dough with half of the cheese cubes and press them into the dough (see page 15). Then allow 4 hours for the final rise. The dough will bubble up around the cheese and rise significantly in the pan.

CONTINUED >

Twenty minutes before assembling and baking the pizza, preheat the oven to 500°F (450°F for convection). When ready to bake, cover the dough with an even layer of Canadian bacon, capicola, or bacon pieces and sprinkle with the onion and jalapeño (if using). Top the dough with the remaining half of the cheese cubes, making sure to get plenty around the edges, where the dough meets the pan. For a 9-inch pan, spread about 3 ounces of the pineapple pieces or slices (the actual amount will depend on the size of the pan) evenly over the cheese.

Bake on the middle shelf of the oven for 8 minutes. Then rotate the pan 180 degrees and continue to bake 7 to 9 minutes longer, or until the cheese caramelizes to a golden brown and the pineapple bubbles and browns or chars slightly.

Transfer the baked pizza to the stovetop or to a heatproof counter. Using an offset spatula or bench blade, carefully slide it around the edge, between the crust and the side of the pan, and then lift the pizza out of the pan and slide it onto a cutting board. Use a spoon or squirt bottle to drizzle the pizzas with the pizza sauce, if using. Garnish with the parsley. Let cool for 1 minute, then cut into 3- or 4-inch squares and serve.

GARLIC LOVERS' ITALIAN SAUSAGE

I can still recall the first time I experienced hot, spicy Italian sausage, even though it was over sixty years ago. The first time I bit into that sausage, the whole pieces of fennel seed, an exotic licorice-like spice, seemed to explode in my mouth. The piquant cayenne- and fennel-infused pork juices imparted a flavor so unexpected and new to me that I became instantly and forever hooked. I was just nine years old at the time, but I know that my craving for spicy sausage began at that moment and has not let up since.

This recipe captures some of that magic in a familiar sausage pizza but in a deep-pan version. You can substitute any favorite sausage, mild or spicy. I often use Creole-style chaurice, or Cajun andouille, or Spanish chorizo, which is different from Mexican chorizo (but which also works). In the end, though, it is that fennel-seeded Italian version that draws me back to those deeply embedded, cherished flavor memories.

As if the Italian sausage were not spicy enough, I have added a layer of thinly sliced fresh garlic under all that cheese and sausage. In my opinion, it raises everything to another level, but be sure your dining companion is also a garlic fan or you may be spending the evening alone. If in doubt, you may omit the garlic. Or, as one of my single friends tells me, find another dining companion (no wonder he's still single). Fortunately for me, my wife loves garlic as much as I do.

Any Master Dough (pages 27–35)

1 pound brick cheese, Muenster, mozzarella, fontina, or provolone cheese (or a combination), cut into ¼-inch cubes (see page 9)

1 pound sweet or hot fresh Italian sausage links

8 to 10 large garlic cloves, peeled and thinly sliced

2 tablespoons olive oil

1 cup Crushed Tomato Pizza Sauce (page 46) or All-Purpose Marinara Pizza Sauce (page 49)

¼ cup chopped flat-leaf parsley, or ¼ teaspoon dried oregano or thyme

Five hours before baking the pizzas, begin panning and dimpling the dough, at 20-minute intervals, as shown on page 13. After three to four rounds of dimpling and resting, the dough will have relaxed enough to cover the whole pan. At this

CONTINUED >

point, top the dough with half of the cheese cubes and press them into the dough (see page 15). Then allow 4 hours for the final rise. The dough will bubble up around the cheese and rise significantly in the pan.

While the dough is rising or up to 1 day before you plan to bake the pizzas, cook the sausage. Preheat the oven to 350°F (325°F for convection) and line a baking sheet with parchment paper. Place the sausage links on the prepared pan and bake on the middle shelf of the oven for 12 to 15 minutes, or until the sausages are firm and springy to the touch. They can be slightly underdone, as they will be cooked again on the pizza. Transfer the pan to a wire rack or trivet and let the sausages cool at room temperature for at least 30 minutes before cutting them crosswise into ¼-inch-thick disks.

While the sausage is cooling, in a small bowl, combine the garlic and the oil and stir until the garlic is coated. Leave the bowl at room temperature until you are ready to assemble the pizzas. (If you are making the oil 1 day ahead, cover the bowl with plastic wrap and refrigerate.)

Twenty minutes before assembling and baking the pizzas, preheat the oven to 500°F (450°F for convection). When ready to bake, cover the dough with the remaining half of the cheese cubes, making sure to get plenty around the edges, where the dough meets the pan. Top the cheese with the garlic slices and drizzle any excess oil in the bowl over the garlic. Cover with the sliced sausage.

Bake on the middle shelf of the oven for 8 minutes. Remove the pan from the oven and lightly drizzle the pizza with pizza sauce. Then rotate the pan 180 degrees, return it to the oven, and bake 7 to 9 minutes longer, or until the cheese and sausage caramelize to a golden brown.

Transfer the baked pizzas to the stovetop or to a heatproof counter. Using an offset spatula or bench blade, carefully slide it around the edge of each pizza, between the crust and the side of the pan, and then lift the pizzas out of the pan and slide them onto a cutting board. Garnish with the parsley or dried oregano or thyme. Let cool for 1 minute, then cut into 3- or 4-inch squares and serve.

Deep-pan pizzas can also be baked in round cake pans.

CHAPTER 4

FOCACCIA, SCHIACCIATA, SICILIAN-STYLE, AND ROMAN-STYLE PIZZAS

Unlike the deep-pan pizzas in the previous chapter, the pizzas in this chapter are designed to be made in a standard sheet pan (home oven-size sheet pans are typically 12 by 17 by 1 inch), though you can also use round cake pans. While the various names and nuances of each style do differentiate them (especially for people from the various regions of Italy), for our purposes they all fall within the category of 1-inch-high pan pizzas rather than the 2- or 3-inch-high pizzas of the deep-pan category. Are these distinctions the result of some bureaucratic pizza rules? No. In fact, we've all seen focaccia and Sicilian-style pizzas as tall as 3 inches, but I just don't like them that way.

This raises another question that I suspect many of you have: can the deep-pan concepts work on the focaccia or Roman-style pizzas and vice versa? I will answer this in two ways: First, there are no pizza police governing these styles; they are your pizzas and you can do whatever you like with them. Second, as long as you exercise a little common sense and don't overload your pizzas with too many toppings, you are free to mix and match and create your own variations at will. The flavor rule will guide you.

While the ingredients listed for all the pizzas in this chapter are scaled for a standard home oven-size sheet pan, if you are using a round cake pan or other type of pan, adjust the amounts accordingly (see page 15 for a chart of dough amounts for various pan sizes).

FOCACCIA AND SCHIACCIATA

Northern Italian focaccia should be every bit as popular in this country as round Neapolitan pizza, but it isn't for one simple reason: it is rarely made well here. The proliferation of bad or, at best, mediocre quick-rising focaccia bread that is so often found in supermarkets and even in restaurants has pretty much ruined the reputation of focaccia for most Americans. One of my goals in this chapter is to reverse that trend and restore focaccia and its Tuscan sibling, *schiacciata*, to the exalted status they deserve.

From my American perspective (please forgive me, all you Italian-food experts), focaccia and schiacciata are simply Ligurian and Tuscan terms for the same product: dough with something on it, usually (but not always) baked in a pan. In Genoa, the spiritual if not actual birthplace of focaccia, people might argue this point, as might the folks in Tuscany, home of schiacciata. I don't really care, though, because we are going to create our own versions, not theirs, though ours will be inspired by the templates for "dough with something on it" that were originally established in these regions. They can be savory or, as you will see, also sweet. Either way, unless you've already been to the great focaccerias of Liguria, these will change your perception of focaccia forever.

FOCACCIA BIANCA WITH HERB OIL

MAKES 1 SHEET PAN OR 2 TO 3 ROUND FOCACCIA

This is the most basic and, many say, still the best version of focaccia, unadorned with toppings other than flavorful herb oil. It can be eaten as is, dipped into marinara sauce, or used as an accompaniment with pretty much any dish. What I love about it is that it showcases the beauty and delicious flavor complexity of the dough, demonstrating why the greatest joy derived from pizza is found in the crust, not the toppings. When properly made, the internal structure of each slice will have a honeycombed, shiny appearance and a soft, creamy texture, sandwiched between a crackly, toasty under-crust and a flavorful thin-but-chewy top crust.

3 tablespoons olive oil, plus more for dimpling

Any Master Dough (pages 27–35)

½ to ¾ cup Herb Oil (page 54), plus more as needed

2 cups freshly grated Parmesan, Romano, or Asiago cheese (optional)

Five hours before baking the focaccia, line the pan with parchment paper or a silicone baking mat and oil the bottom and interior sides with the 3 tablespoons olive oil. Begin panning and dimpling the dough, at 20-minute intervals, as shown on page 13, dipping your fingers in olive oil to keep them from sticking to the dough as you work. After three to four rounds of dimpling and resting, the dough will have relaxed enough to cover the whole pan. At this point, drizzle the dough with ½ cup of the Herb Oil and dimple it into the dough, spreading it with your fingers to evenly coat the surface of the dough as it fills the entire pan. Cover the pan loosely with plastic wrap. Then allow 4 hours for the final rise.

When the dough reaches the rim of the pan (or doubled in height, if using round cake pans), preheat the oven to 475°F (425°F for convection). Carefully peel off the plastic wrap. The dough will be airy and bubbly. If it seems as though the Herb Oil has been absorbed and is invisible in some areas, use a tablespoon to drizzle additional Herb Oil over those areas where it seems sparse (but without additional dimpling).

CONTINUED >

Bake on the middle shelf of the oven for 8 minutes. Then rotate the pan 180 degrees and bake 9 to 12 minutes longer, or until the top and the undercrust are golden brown. If using cheese, remove the pan from the oven when the focaccia looks done and sprinkle it with the cheese. Return the pan to the oven for 2 minutes and then remove it.

Transfer the baked focaccia to the stovetop or to a heatproof counter. Using an offset spatula or bench blade, carefully slide it around the edge, between the crust and the side of the pan, and then lift the focaccia out of the pan and slide it onto a cutting board. Drizzle any oil remaining in the baking pan over the focaccia. If the parchment paper or baking mat is still clinging to the focaccia, remove it. Let cool for 5 minutes, then cut into 3- or 4-inch squares and serve.

FOCACCIA ROSSA (RED VARIATION)

Replace the Herb Oil with 1 to 1½ cups of either the Crushed Tomato Pizza Sauce (page 46) or All-Purpose Marinara Pizza Sauce (page 49). Just before baking, drizzle the sauce over the dough and gently spread it over the top with a pastry brush or the back of a tablespoon. Bake as described for the Bianca, but allow an extra 4 to 5 minutes of baking time to cook the dough under the sauce.

BLUE CHEESE, BALSAMIC ONION MARMALADE, AND WALNUT FOCCACCIA

MAKES 1 SHEET PAN OR 2 TO 3 ROUND FOCACCIA

This is probably my most well-known and popular focaccia creation. It is also my personal favorite and one of the best things I've ever eaten. The three toppings are each excellent and sufficient unto themselves, but somehow, together, they create a flavor synergy that is far greater than the sum of their parts. The balsamic onion marmalade should be made in advance; it can take up to 45 minutes to prepare it properly. You also might want to double or triple the batch; I've published other versions of this focaccia in my previous books, and many readers tell me that the onion marmalade recipe alone was worth the price of the book and something they make often. For the blue cheese, I suggest a young, firm one (not the precrumbled kind), not a ripe, mealy piece, which is too difficult to break into smaller crumbles and also tends to exert too strong an influence on the overall flavor balance. It doesn't matter whether you use Gorgonzola, Danish, or domestic blue; just be sure it's firm and easy to crumble. Because it will be getting baked amid the onions and walnuts, this is not the time to use a super expensive blue cheese like Roquefort or Stilton; an everyday blue is more than sufficient. Always put the walnut (or pecan) pieces on the dough first so that you can cover them with the balsamic onions and then the blue cheese. The onions will protect the nuts, so that they don't burn during the bake. Note that the onions aren't fully caramelized when you first make them; they are merely softened and lightly browned so that they release their juices, which become a glaze as they reduce. The brown color is, initially, imparted by the balsamic vinegar. Later, when you bake the focaccia, the onions will fully caramelize and become almost as sweet as candy, mellowing the pungency of the blue cheese.

3 tablespoons plus 1 teaspoon olive oil, plus more for dimpling

Any Master Dough (pages 27–35)

1¼ cups walnuts or pecans, very coarsely chopped

2 cups Carmelized Balsamic Onion Marmalade (page 56)

1 cup coarsely crumbled firm blue cheese

CONTINUED >

Five hours before baking the focaccia, line the pan with parchment paper or a silicone baking mat and oil the bottom and interior sides with the 3 tablespoons olive oil. Begin panning and dimpling the dough, at 20-minute intervals, as shown on page 13, dipping your fingers in olive oil to keep them from sticking to the dough as you work. After three to four rounds of dimpling and resting, the dough will have relaxed enough to cover the whole pan. At this point, rub the remaining 1 teaspoon of oil over the dough and cover the pan loosely with plastic wrap. Then allow 4 hours for the final rise.

When the dough reaches the rim of the pan (or doubled in size, if using round cake pans), preheat the oven to 475°F (425°F for convection). Carefully peel off the plastic wrap and top the dough with the walnuts, pressing them into the dough. Spread the onion marmalade over the dough. Then top with the blue cheese, spacing the crumbles evenly so that every piece of the focaccia will include a pocket of blue cheese as well as walnuts and onions.

Bake on the middle shelf of the oven for 8 minutes. Then rotate the pan 180 degrees and bake 10 to 12 minutes longer, or until the edge of the focaccia is golden brown and the dough is springy when poked in the center. The undercrust of the focaccia as well as the onions should be caramelized to a golden brown.

Transfer the baked focaccia to the stovetop or to a heatproof counter. Using an offset spatula or bench blade, carefully slide it around the edge, between the crust and the side of the pan, and then lift the focaccia out of the pan and slide it onto a cutting board. If the parchment paper or baking mat is still clinging to the focaccia, remove it. Let cool for 5 minutes, then cut into 3- or 4-inch squares and serve.

HERBED TOMATO AND PESTO FOCACCIA

MAKES 1 SHEET PAN OR 2 TO 3 ROUND FOCACCIA

At the end of my focaccia classes, we take a vote as to which ones were the class favorites. The vote is usually very close between this one and the Blue Cheese, Balsamic Onion Marmalade, and Walnut Focaccia. Same dough but two totally different flavor experiences, and both of them amazing! The flavors are enhanced by the use of Herb Oil to marinate the sliced plum tomatoes before they top the focaccia. You can use the leftover Herb Oil and tomato juices as a dip or condiment. Serve in a bowl for dipping or drizzle over the top of the focaccia.

I have left the best part for last: fresh basil pesto is drizzled over the tomatoes after the focaccia comes out of the oven. The pesto serves two purposes: not only is it a delicious complement to the tomatoes but its bright green color also provides a beautiful contrast to the orange and brown earth tones of the baked tomatoes and caramelized crust. Yes, eye appeal is important, but beautiful presentations can only support, and not take precedence over, the most important aspect of the dish: its flavor. This focaccia is a winner on both fronts.

3 tablespoons plus 1 teaspoon olive oil, plus more for dimpling	1 cup Herb Oil (page 54), made with additional 1 teaspoon dried basil, or 3 tablespoons minced fresh basil	8 Roma or other plum tomatoes, cut into ¼-inch-thick slices
Any Master Dough (pages 27–35)		1 cup Pesto Genovese (page 51)

Five hours before baking the focaccia, line the pan with parchment paper or a silicone baking mat and oil the bottom and interior sides with the 3 tablespoons olive oil. Begin panning and dimpling the dough, at 20-minute intervals, as shown on page 13, dipping your fingers in olive oil to keep them from sticking to the dough as you work. After three to four rounds of dimpling and resting, the dough will have relaxed enough to cover the whole pan. At this point, rub the remaining 1 teaspoon of oil over the dough and cover the pan loosely with plastic wrap. Then allow 4 hours for the final rise.

While the dough is rising, prepare the Herb Oil, adding the dried or fresh basil listed to that called for in the oil recipe. Place the tomato slices in a bowl, pour the Herb Oil over the tomatoes, and with your hands, toss the tomatoes in the oil until evenly coated.

When the dough has risen to the rim of the pan (or doubled in height, if using round cake pans), completely cover the dough by arranging the tomatoes end to end. If there are tomato pieces left, place them over any areas between the tomato slices where the dough is showing through. (You can also cut them to fit these gaps.) Save the remaining Herb Oil, along with any residual tomato juice.

Preheat the oven to 475°F (425°F for convection). Bake the focaccia on the middle shelf of the oven for 10 minutes. Then rotate the pan 180 degrees and continue baking 12 to 15 minutes longer, until the tomatoes are slightly charred and the visible focaccia crust is golden brown and springy to the touch. (Note: This foccacia takes longer to bake than many of the others because of the tomatoes.) The undercrust of the focaccia should also be caramelized to a golden brown.

Transfer the baked focaccia to the stovetop or to a heatproof counter. Using an offset spatula or bench blade, carefully slide it around the edge, between the crust and the side of the pan, and then lift the focaccia out of the pan and slide it onto a cutting board. Use a tablespoon to drizzle the pesto over the focaccia in streaks, so that the tomatoes peek through. Let cool for 5 minutes, then cut into 3- or 4-inch squares and serve.

BACON AND POTATO FOCACCIA

MAKES 1 SHEET PAN OR 2 TO 3 ROUND FOCACCIA

Potato focaccia is one of the most popular and traditional of pizza variations, both in the United States and in Italy, but we're going to add a couple of special tweaks, including the use of Herb Oil and bacon to push the flavor profile beyond what you've probably had before. Use the thinnest slicing attachment on your food processor, or use a mandolin, which can be found at most cookware stores. It's difficult to achieve paper-thin potato slices with a knife, so if you choose that option, you should blanch the slices for about 60 seconds. Regardless of how you prepare the potatoes, coat and cover them with Herb Oil, which will enhance their flavor and help crisp them up.

This focaccia can also be made without the bacon, but for us bacon lovers, that would be what we'd call a Plan B. If you go that route, sprinkle an additional layer of Parmesan cheese under the potato layer to replace the bacon.

3 tablespoons plus 1 teaspoon olive oil, plus more for dimpling	2 large or 3 medium-size Yukon Gold potatoes, washed but not peeled	½ teaspoon salt, plus more as needed
Any Master Dough (pages 27–35)	1 cup Herb Oil (page 54), made with an additional 1 teaspoon dried or fresh rosemary	1 cup freshly grated Parmesan, Romano, or Asiago cheese
8 ounces sliced bacon		

Five hours before baking the focaccia, line the pan with parchment paper or a silicone baking mat and oil the bottom and interior sides with the 3 tablespoons of olive oil. Begin panning and dimpling the dough, at 20-minute intervals, as shown on page 13, dipping your fingers in olive oil to keep them from sticking to the dough as you work. After three to four rounds of dimpling and resting, the dough will have relaxed enough to cover the whole pan. At this point, rub the remaining 1 teaspoon of oil over the dough and cover the pan loosely with plastic wrap. Then allow 4 hours for the final rise.

Preheat the oven to 375°F (350°F for convection). Arrange the bacon strips in a single layer on a sheet pan and bake for 12 to 18 minutes, or until the bacon is crisp. Set the pan aside to cool, leaving the strips in the bacon fat.

Using a mandolin or the slicer blade of a food processor, slice the potatoes into very thin disks. If using a knife, first cut the potatoes in half so that they will lay flat and then cut crosswise into very thin half disks, ⅛ inch thick or even thinner if possible. If the potatoes are sliced with a knife, blanch them in a quart of boiling water with the salt for 30 to 60 seconds, then drain and pat dry with paper towels. Add the potato slices to the Herb Oil and stir them, using your fingers to separate the slices so that all are fully coated. Cover the bowl and set it aside.

When the dough has risen to the rim of the pan (or doubled in height, if using round cake pans), chop the bacon into ½-inch pieces (any bacon fat that stays with the bacon is a bonus), and sprinkle them evenly over the dough. Cover the bacon with a single layer of the oiled potato slices, overlapping them slightly, domino-style, so that they completely cover the dough. Any extra potato slices can be used as a second layer around the outer edge. Dot the potatoes with the remaining bacon fat (optional).

Preheat the oven to 475°F (425°F for convection). Bake on the middle shelf of the oven for 8 minutes. Then rotate the pan 180 degrees and bake 10 to 12 minutes longer, or until the potatoes turn a rich golden brown and crisp around the edges. Remove the pan from the oven and sprinkle the potatoes with the grated cheese. Return the pan to the oven and bake 2 to 4 minutes longer, or until the cheese melts and begins to caramelize.

Transfer the baked focaccia to the stovetop or to a heatproof counter. Using an offset spatula or bench blade, carefully slide it around the edge, between the crust and the side of the pan, and then lift the focaccia out of the pan and slide it onto a cutting board. If the parchment paper or baking mat is still clinging to the focaccia, remove it. Let cool for 5 minutes, then cut into 3- or 4-inch squares and serve.

FRUITED FOCACCIA WITH CITRUS GLAZE

MAKES 1 SHEET PAN OR 3 ROUND FOCACCIA

This fruit-studded stunner has the appeal of an enriched morning pastry, like a Danish. What I especially love about this focaccia is that it can be served for breakfast, for dessert, or even for an afterschool snack. It's an anytime treat! While my favorite fruit combination is half golden raisins and half dried cranberries, any dried fruit will work if you want to mix it up a bit. Because the dried fruit needs to plump up in the dough, you have to add extra water when you mix it, as you will see in the following recipe instructions. The dough will seem way too wet at first, but during the overnight cold fermentation, the fruit will absorb much of the liquid, so that the dough will firm up and feel like regular Master Dough when you pan it the following day.

The Citrus Glaze is easy to make and really highlights the flavors of the fruits, but it is totally optional (I love it!). If you'd prefer to omit it, simply brush the top of the baked focaccia with olive oil as soon as it comes out of the oven to shine it up.

NOTE: *Rather than make one large sheet-pan focaccia, you can also divide the dough into three pieces to be baked in 10-inch round cake pans. If you want to bake only one such focaccia, you can put the other two pieces in oiled resealable freezer bags and freeze them for future use. To use this dough from the freezer, simply transfer the bag to the refrigerator the day before you plan to bake so that it can slowly thaw and soften. You can then treat it just as you would overnight refrigerated dough.*

Ingredients for one batch any Master Dough (pages 27–35)	¾ cup golden or dark raisins	3 tablespoons plus 1 teaspoon olive oil, plus more as needed
½ cup plus 2 tablespoons (142 g) cool water	¾ cup dried cranberries, cherries, apricots, or other dried fruit	Citrus Glaze (recipe follows)

Following the recipe for any Master Dough, mix the dough ingredients, adding the ½ cup plus 2 tablespoons (142 g) water, raisins, and dried fruit. At this point, the dough will be too wet and sticky to stretch and fold, so after mixing, place it in an oiled bowl, cover it with plastic wrap, and refrigerate for 12 to 48 hours.

Five hours before baking the focaccia, line a sheet pan or cake pans with parchment paper or a silicone baking mat and oil the bottom and interior sides with 3 tablespoons of the oil. For a 12 by 17-inch sheet pan, use 3 pounds (1.36 kg) of the dough. For round focaccia, use one-third of the dough (about 1 pound) for each 10-inch round cake pan.

Stretch and fold the dough in the bowl (the dough will have firmed up considerably as the fruit absorbs some of the moisture). Begin panning and dimpling the dough, at 20-minute intervals, as shown on page 13. After the third or fourth dimpling, the dough will have relaxed enough to cover the whole pan. Brush the dough with the remaining teaspoon of oil and loosely cover the pan with plastic wrap. Then allow 4 hours for the final rise.

While the dough is rising, make the Citrus Glaze. When the dough has fully risen, you can either bake the focaccia, or if you prefer serving it hot for breakfast, refrigerate the dough overnight and remove it 1 hour before baking.

Preheat the oven to 450°F (400°F for convection). Bake the focaccia on the middle shelf of the oven for 12 minutes. Then rotate the pan 180 degrees and bake 10 to 12 minutes longer. Both the top and the undercrust should be a dark golden brown and caramelized.

Transfer the baked focaccia to the stovetop or to a heatproof counter. Using an offset spatula or bench blade, carefully slide it around the edge, between the crust and the side of the pan, and then lift the focaccia out of the pan and slide it onto a cutting board. Use a rubber or icing spatula to spread the glaze evenly over the focaccia. Let the glazed focaccia cool for at least 5 minutes, then cut into 3- or 4-inch squares and serve warm. The focaccia can also be served at room temperature, after the glaze has fully dried.

CITRUS GLAZE
MAKES 1 CUP

2 cups confectioners' sugar, sifted	½ teaspoon orange or lemon extract, 2 teaspoons thawed orange juice concentrate, 2 teaspoons lemon juice, or 1 tablespoon orange liqueur or limoncello	4 to 6 tablespoons water or milk, plus more as needed

In a small mixing bowl, whisk together the sugar and orange or lemon flavorings. Add 4 tablespoons of water or milk and continue whisking to make a smooth, spreadable paste. Add more liquid, by the teaspoon, if necessary, to reach a consistency of thick gravy. The glaze will keep in the refrigerator for up to 2 weeks.

GRAPE AND ANISE SCHIACCIATA

MAKES TWO 10-INCH OR 12-INCH ROUND OR THREE 8-INCH OR 9-INCH SCHIACCIATA

So why is this a *schiacciata* and not a focaccia? Simply because I first ran across a similar version during a trip to Tuscany, where it was called *schiacciata* and not focaccia. And, unlike the other focaccia recipes in this chapter, which I usually prefer to bake in rectangular sheet pans, I like this fruited pan pizza (okay, *schiacciata*) best when it's baked in round cake pans, where the tall sides of the pans are much more conducive than shallow-rimmed sheet pans to containing and enveloping the sweet, juicy grape and anise filling. By whatever name you call it, or shape in which you bake it, this flavorful *schiacciata* is something very special.

8 to 10 tablespoons olive oil, plus more as needed

Any Master Dough (pages 27–35)

4 cups seedless or pitted grapes or whole currants (halved if large)

1 teaspoon whole anise seeds

4 tablespoons brown sugar

¼ cup water

½ cup granulated sugar

4 tablespoons anise liqueur (such as Sambuca, Pernod, or anisette) or orange liqueur

Five hours before baking the *schiacciata*, line two 10- to 12-inch round or three 8- or 9-inch round cake pans with paper parchment or silicone baking mats and oil the bottom and interior sides of each pan with 3 tablespoons of the oil. Oil a regular sheet pan with 1 tablespoon of oil. If using 10- to 12-inch cake pans, divide your dough into 4 equal pieces of about 9 ounces (255 g) each. If using 8- to 9-inch cake pans, divide your dough into 6 equal pieces of about 6 ounces (170 g) each. Form each piece into a loose ball.

Place 1 piece of dough in each pan. Place the remaining dough pieces on the prepared sheet pan, brush each piece with oil, and cover loosely with plastic wrap. Begin panning and dimpling the dough, at 20-minute intervals, as shown on page 13. After three to four rounds of dimpling and resting, the dough will have relaxed enough to cover the whole pan. At this point, divide the grapes between the pans, pressing them into the dough. In a small bowl, mix together the anise seeds and the brown sugar and sprinkle the mixture evenly over the grapes. Cover each pan with a disk of the remaining dough, stretching each as you would a pizza dough and laying it over the top of the grapes. Crimp it to the lower piece with

CONTINUED >

your fingers, working around the interior edge of the pan. Brush each top with 1 tablespoon of the oil and cover the pans loosely with plastic wrap. Then, allow 4 hours for the final rise.

While the dough is rising, combine the water, granulated sugar, and liqueur in a small saucepan and bring to a boil. Lower the heat and simmer, stirring, for 3 to 5 minutes, until reduced to the consistency of maple syrup or honey. Remove the pan from the heat and set it aside to cool.

Preheat the oven to 450°F (425°F for convection). Cut a few vent holes in the top of the dough to release steam while baking. Bake on the middle shelf of the oven for 10 minutes. Then rotate the pans 180 degrees and continue baking 10 to 14 minutes longer, or until both the tops and the undercrust are golden brown and caramelized.

Transfer the baked *schiacciatas* to the stovetop or to a heatproof counter and let cool for 10 minutes. While they are cooling, brush the top crust with the sugar syrup. Using an offset spatula or bench blade, carefully slide it around the edge, between the crust and the side of the pan, and then lift the *schiacciatas* out of the pan and slide them onto a cutting board. If the parchment or baking mat is still clinging to the *schiacciata*, remove it. While the *schiacciatas* are still warm, brush the top crust again with sugar syrup. Let cool for at least 5 minutes, then cut into wedges and serve.

SICILIAN-STYLE AND GRANDMA PIZZA

Sicilian-style and Grandma pies are both variations of pan pizza, closer to focaccia than to the Detroit-style deep-pan pizza. In fact, Sicilian-style or Grandma pizza might just as easily be called focaccia. Both are extensions of and have been inspired by Ligurian focaccia as well as by Neapolitan sauce-and-cheese pizzas. Unlike focaccia, however, these two styles of pizza have not been ruined in this country, mainly because they were basically invented here, in Italian American communities like New York City's Brooklyn and Queens. There are a number of pizzerias doing splendid jobs with these styles, and many of us have fond childhood taste memories associated with them. There is, in fact, very little difference between Sicilian-style and Grandma pizza, though advocates for one or the other may disagree with me. But from what I've seen and tasted, the main difference is that a Grandma pizza is baked once, whereas a Sicilian-style is baked twice and has a slightly thicker crust. This distinction may be arguable (I've seen definitions that describe them in opposite terms). Sicilian-style pizza weighs in at 32 ounces (907 g) and is double baked, while our Grandma variation is also 32 ounces (907 g) but baked only once. Which one you prefer will be, as it is with all pizza, a very personal matter. I suggest, however, that you make both types in order to properly arrive at this very difficult decision. Regardless of which side you land on, it will be a fun and enjoyable journey.

HOW TO PAN AND PAR-BAKE A SICILIAN-STYLE CRUST

The Sicilian-style pizza is the only one in this book whose crust is partially baked in advance. Once the crust is baked, it becomes very stable and won't buckle under the weight of sauce and toppings. This is what makes it more like a focaccia than like a Neapolitan pizza even though the toppings are more generous than in the Neapolitan style. Make the full recipe for Master Dough (36 ounces/1.021 kg), the same as you would for focaccia, but scale it to 32 ounces when it comes time to pan the dough. You can save the excess dough and form it into a roll or make a mini pizza, or refrigerate it and add it to the next batch of dough.

At least 3 hours before you plan to bake the pizza (or even a day or two ahead), oil a 12 by 17-inch sheet pan, including the interior sides, with 3 tablespoons of the olive oil. Place the portioned dough in the pan and dimple it, at 20-minute intervals, as shown on page 13, dipping your fingers in olive oil to keep them from sticking to the dough as you work. After three to four rounds of dimpling and resting, the dough will have relaxed enough to cover the whole pan. Loosely cover the pan with plastic wrap, then allow 2 hours for the final rise. Unlike the procedure for focaccia, we don't wait for the dough to get super airy and bubbly or to rise all the way to the top of the pan.

CONTINUED >

After a 2-hour rise, preheat the oven to 500°F (450°F for convection). Brush the surface of the pizza with an additional tablespoon of olive oil and give it a final, gentle dimpling through the middle—but not at the perimeter—of the pizza. Place the pan on the middle shelf of the oven, and bake for 5 minutes. Then rotate the pan 180 degrees and bake 5 minutes longer, or until the dough is slightly firm and springy to the touch and just lightly browned and caramelized. It will spring up as it bakes and might even reach close to the top of the pan and form a rim by the time it's done, but it will have a cell structure different from that of a fully raised focaccia. At this point, remove the pan from the oven and set it aside to cool. You can also top it and return it to the oven immediately, if you prefer.

Notes

- If you are making a red sauce pizza, you have the option of brushing a thin layer of the pizza sauce over the surface for the par-bake (as we do for the Focaccia Rossa, page 126) and then using a second round of sauce during the final bake. You can make a Sicilian-style pizza with or without this additional step, so you may want to try it both ways to see which approach you prefer.

- Another key to the success of this dough is the generous use of olive oil for greasing the pan. Remember to line the pan first with either parchment paper or a silicone baking mat (Silpat) and then spread 4 tablespoons of olive oil over the surface and also on the inside walls of the pan. This oil is what creates the "buttered toast" effect on the undercrust as it essentially fries it. Along with long fermentation and the high hydration of the dough, this is another source of the "magic" of a great pan pizza.

- Instead of cutting the cheese into cubes as we do for Detroit-style deep-pan pizza, for Sicilian-style pizza, we grate or shred it. We do this because the cheese doesn't go on until the second bake, so it has less time to fully melt than it would have on a deep-pan pizza.

Baked Sicilian-style crusts, from the top: Naturally Leavened Dough, Whole Grain Country-Style Dough, and White Flour Dough

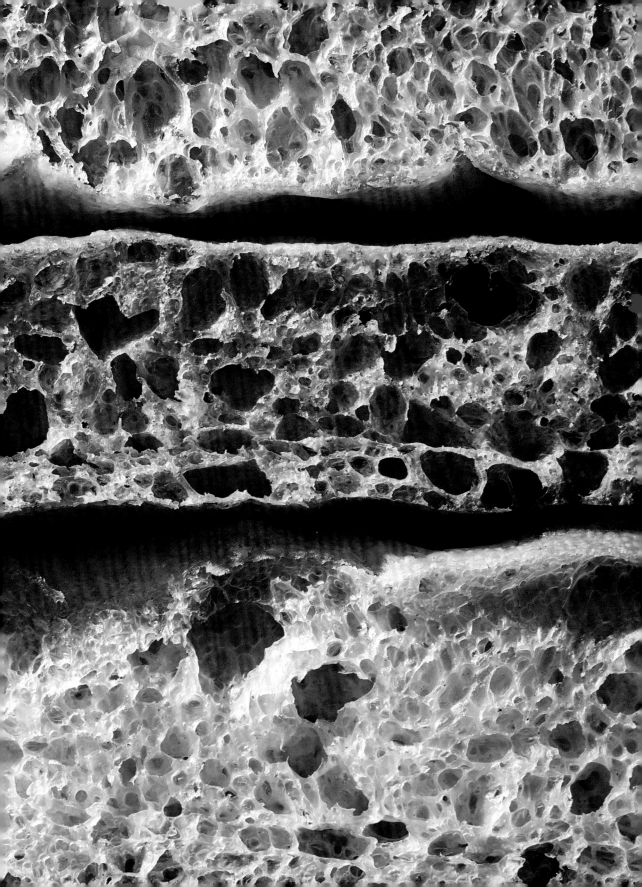

CLASSIC PEPPERONI

MAKES ONE 12 BY 17-INCH SICILIAN-STYLE PIZZA

Once again, we are back to pepperoni land, a place very hard to avoid because pepperoni works so well on pizza. And, if you like your pepperoni pizza straight up, on a simple sauce-and-cheese Sicilian-style pizza, this is as easy as it gets. (Or, for a more embellished version, take a look at the deep-pan Pepperoni Deluxe Pizza on page 75, which can be applied to this variation.) Either way, the rubrics are simple: a twice-baked dough with plenty of cheese and Crushed Tomato Pizza Sauce double topped with pepperoni slices. Some people think that to do anything else to this pizza is like gilding the lily and, while I'm partial to having mine with pickled peppers, they might be right.

32 ounces (907 g) of any Master Dough (pages 27–35)

5 tablespoons olive oil

1 teaspoon red pepper flakes (optional)

1½ cups Crushed Tomato Pizza Sauce (page 46) or All-Purpose Marinara Pizza Sauce (page 49)

4 ounces pepperoni, cut crosswise into thin slices

4 cups grated or shredded mozzarella, provolone, or fontina cheese

¼ cup freshly grated Parmesan, Asiago, or Romano cheese

1 teaspoon finely chopped fresh oregano, or ¼ teaspoon dried oregano

Follow the instructions for panning and par-baking Sicilian-style dough (see page 139).

Twenty minutes before baking the actual pizza, preheat the oven to 500°F (450°F for convection). Stir the pepper flakes into the pizza sauce. Ladle the sauce over the par-baked crust, then cover the sauce with half of the pepperoni. Top with the mozzarella or other soft cheese (not the Parmesan or dried cheese) and add another layer of the remaining pepperoni.

Bake on the middle shelf of the oven for 6 minutes. Then rotate the pan 180 degrees and bake 5 to 7 minutes longer, or until the cheese is melted and golden and the pepperoni is crisp. Remove the pan from the oven and sprinkle the pizza with the grated Parmesan (or other dried cheese). Return the pizza to the oven for 1 minute to slightly melt the dried cheese.

Transfer the baked pizza to the stovetop or to a heatproof counter and let cool for 2 minutes. Using an offset spatula or bench blade, carefully slide it around the edge, between the crust and the side of the pan, and then lift the pizza out of the pan and slide it onto a cutting board. Sprinkle the pizza with fresh or dried oregano then cut into 3- or 4-inch squares and serve.

UMBERTO'S-STYLE GRANDMA PIE

MAKES ONE 12 BY 17-INCH PIZZA

Umberto's, in New Hyde Park, Queens, is famous for this style of pizza (as is another place in Queens called, confusingly, Prince Umberto's), but these sheet-pan pizzas have been made under various names for many years in many cities. The main difference between a Grandma and a Sicilian-style pizza, at least by some definitions, is that the Grandma pie is baked just once, with all the toppings on board, and not par-baked and then topped. This does create some challenges, such as getting the crust to finish baking at the same time as the toppings, so this is accomplished by first layering sliced, not grated, mozzarella cheese over the surface, not overloading the pizza with too much sauce, and baking at a slightly lower temperature and on a lower shelf in the oven, where the undercrust can bake before the cheese gets too well done. As always, it comes down to a balancing act between time, temperature, and ingredients.

NOTE: *You can always add pepperoni or other toppings to this pizza, as you would for the Sicilian-style pizza. If not using fresh mozzarella, increase the grated mozzarella to 4 cups.*

---

5 tablespoons olive oil

32 ounces (907 g) of any Master Dough (pages 27–35)

4 garlic cloves, finely diced

1¼ cups Crushed Tomato Pizza Sauce (page 46) or All-Purpose Marinara Pizza Sauce (page 49)

6 ounces full-fat mozzarella cheese, thinly sliced

3 ounces fresh mozzarella cheese (optional)

¼ cup freshly grated Parmesan, Asiago, or Romano cheese

1 teaspoon chopped fresh oregano or ¼ teaspoon dried oregano

At least 3 hours before you plan to bake the pizza, oil a 12 by 17-inch sheet pan, including the interior sides, with 4 tablespoons of the oil (you can use a pan liner, but it is not required). Begin panning and dimpling the dough, at 20-minute intervals, as shown on page 13. After three to four rounds of dimpling and resting, the dough will have relaxed enough to cover the whole pan. At this point, coat the top with the remaining 1 tablespoon of oil and sprinkle with the garlic. Cover the pan with plastic wrap and let it rest for 2 to 2½ hours at room temperature.

CONTINUED >

Twenty minutes before baking the pizza, preheat the oven to 450°F (425°F for convection). Remove the plastic wrap and lay the sliced mozzarella cheese over the surface, covering it as completely as possible. Ladle and spread the sauce over the cheese. If using, tear or cut the fresh mozzarella into 8 to 10 pieces and space them evenly over the sauce.

Bake on a shelf in the lower third of the oven for 8 minutes. Then rotate the pan 180 degrees and continue baking 8 to 12 minutes longer, or until the cheese is bubbly and caramelized and the undercrust is brown and crisp. Remove the pan from the oven and sprinkle the pizza with the grated Parmesan or other dried cheese. Return the pizza to the oven for 1 minute to slightly melt the cheese.

Transfer the baked pizza to the stovetop or to a heatproof counter and let it rest for 2 minutes. Using an offset spatula or bench blade, carefully slide it around the edge, between the crust and the side of the pan, and then lift the pizza out of the pan and slide it onto a cutting board. Sprinkle the pizza with oregano, then cut into 3- or 4-inch squares and serve. (Note: You can also cut the pizza directly in the pan if it is too difficult to remove, but be careful not to cut into the metal of the pan.)

SPICY AMATRICIANA

MAKES ONE 12 BY 17-INCH SICILIAN-STYLE PIZZA

Amatrice is a region in central Italy where a lot of superb meat and cheese products are produced, and is especially known for its famous pasta sauce called *sugo*. One version of the sauce is known as *salsa all'amatriciana*, which is made with guanciale (cured and spiced pork cheek), locally produced pecorino sheep's milk cheese, San Marzano tomatoes, white wine, black pepper, and chile peppers. Guanciale, while not technically bacon, tastes and cooks like bacon (I think of it as bacon on crack), so if you can't get your hands on any guanciale (see Resources, page 175), feel free to use either pancetta or slab bacon. Another nice touch is the fresh goat cheese (or other creamy cheese) as a refreshing counterpoint to the spicy sauce and bacon. There's a lot going on in this unique, spicy pie (and notice there's no mozzarella or melting cheese), but it's definitely worth the ride.

32 ounces (907 g) of any Master Dough (pages 27–35)

8 ounces guanciale, pancetta, or slab bacon, cut into ½-inch cubes

¼ cup dry white wine

1½ cups Crushed Tomato Pizza Sauce (page 46) or All-Purpose Marinara Pizza Sauce (page 49)

1 teaspoon red pepper flakes

1 cup freshly grated Romano, Parmesan, or Asiago cheese

1 cup crumbled fresh goat cheese, crescenza, mascarpone, or ricotta

2 teaspoons fresh oregano leaves, or ½ teaspoon dried oregano

Follow the instructions for panning and par-baking Sicilian-style dough (see page 139).

While the dough is rising, cook the cubed guanciale in a large frying pan over medium-high heat until most of the fat is rendered and the meat is fully cooked but not totally crisp or caramelized. Using a slotted spoon or strainer, transfer the meat from the melted fat to a bowl and set aside to cool. Save the fat in a separate container.

Preheat the oven to 500°F (450°F for convection). Add the wine to the tomato sauce and stir until blended, then stir in the pepper flakes. Ladle the sauce over the par-baked crust. Top the sauce with the partially cooked guanciale.

Bake on the middle shelf of the oven for 6 minutes. Then rotate the pan 180 degrees and continue baking 5 to 8 minutes longer, or until the meat is crisp and caramelized, and the edge of the crust turns golden brown. Remove the pan from the oven and sprinkle the pizza with the grated Romano cheese. Return the pizza to the oven for 1 minute to lightly melt the cheese.

Transfer the baked pizza to the stovetop or to a heatproof counter. Using an offset spatula or bench blade, carefully slide it around the edge, between the crust and the side of the pan, and then lift the pizza out of the pan and slide it onto a cutting board. Top the pizza with dollops of the goat cheese and sprinkle with the oregano. Let cool for 2 minutes, then cut into 3- or 4-inch squares and serve.

LEMON, SPINACH, AND CHEESE CURD

MAKES ONE 12 BY 17-INCH SICILIAN-STYLE PIZZA

Cheese curds form during the early stage of the cheese-making process, after the milk has separated into curds and whey and the whey is drained off, leaving a giant block of solid curd, which can then be cut or crumbled into smaller pieces. This curd is what gets turned into silky fresh mozzarella balls when put it in a warm bath, or it can be dried and aged to make other cheeses. With a little salt mixed in, curds are delicious by themselves (and are amazing on poutine, the iconic dish of Quebec, Canada, which is made with french fries, cheese curds, and brown gravy). I call cheese curds "squeak cheese," because of the sound they make in your mouth when you chew them. But the point is that while cheese curds look like chunks of firm cottage cheese, they actually melt quite nicely on a pizza, just like fresh mozzarella. This pizza takes advantage of that and marries the melted cheese with delicious lemon-garlic spinach.

I have also made this pizza with fresh greens other than spinach, such as arugula and baby kale, so feel free to substitute. It may look like there's a lot of greens in those 5-ounce plastic containers you find at the supermarket, but they cook down quite a bit by the time the pizza emerges, so fear not. For this recipe, you should wash, drain, and pat dry whichever greens you choose to use.

32 ounces (907 g) of any Master Dough (pages 27–35)

1½ cups Crushed Tomato Pizza Sauce (page 46) or All-Purpose Marinara Pizza Sauce (page 49)

5 ounces baby spinach or other baby greens

5 tablespoons olive oil

3 tablespoons freshly squeezed lemon juice

½ teaspoon kosher salt

⅛ teaspoon freshly ground black pepper

3 garlic cloves, finely chopped, plus more as needed

3 cups fresh, crumbled, or cubed cheese curds, or 8 ounces fresh mozzarella, cut into 1-inch pieces

¼ cup freshly grated Parmesan, Romano, or Asiago cheese

Follow the instructions for panning and par-baking Sicilian-style dough (see page 139).

While the dough is rising, wash and dry the baby spinach. Transfer the spinach to a mixing bowl and toss it with the oil, lemon juice, salt, pepper, and garlic until the spinach is evenly coated.

CONTINUED >

Preheat the oven to 500°F (450°F for convection). Ladle the sauce over the par-baked crust. Spread the dressed spinach over the sauce and top with the cheese curds. Drizzle any remaining dressing from the spinach over the pizza.

Bake on the middle shelf of the oven for 6 minutes. Then rotate the pan 180 degrees and bake 5 to 8 minutes longer, or until the cheese melts, the spinach wilts, and the edge of the crust turns golden brown.

Transfer the baked pizza to the stovetop or to a heatproof counter and let cool for 2 minutes. Using an offset spatula or bench blade, carefully slide it around the edge, between the crust and the side of the pan, and then lift the pizza out of the pan and slide it onto a cutting board. Sprinkle the pizza with the Parmesan cheese, cut into 3- or 4-inch squares, and serve.

WHITE CLAMS CASINO

This pizza is my absolute favorite, whether it's a Frank Pepe's New Haven Neapolitan pie or this original Sicilian-style variation, created just for this book. When I was a kid, my dad's favorite appetizer was something called clams casino, which consisted of whole or chopped clams, Italian herbs, bacon crumbles, a shot of Tabasco, and a small amount of seasoned breadcrumbs. The crumbs were kept to a minimum. Unlike the New England "stuffies" (stuffed clams) I ate when I lived in Providence, Rhode Island, which are way too bready for me, the Philly version had just enough crumbs to hold the mixture together and keep the juices in. For clams casino, everything is packed into a half shell, baked or broiled, and then slurped with great gusto. I think my dad would have flipped over this pizza version of his beloved clams casino. This one is for him.

32 ounces (907 g) of any Master Dough (pages 27–35)

1 cup dried breadcrumbs or Japanese panko

12 ounces bacon, cooked until crisp and then crumbled, fat reserved

13 ounces chopped, minced, or baby clams, in their juice

½ teaspoon dried oregano

¼ teaspoon dried thyme

½ cup chopped basil leaves

4 garlic cloves, finely chopped

1 teaspoon Tabasco or other hot sauce (optional)

⅛ teaspoon freshly ground black pepper

1 tablespoon freshly squeezed lemon juice

Salt

2 cups freshly grated mozzarella, fontina, or provolone cheese

½ cup freshly grated Parmesan, Romano, or Asiago cheese

½ cup chopped flat-leaf parsley

Follow the instructions for panning and par-baking Sicilian-style dough (see page 139).

While the dough is rising, toss the breadcrumbs with 2 tablespoons of the bacon fat in a small bowl and set aside. Drain the clams, reserving the juice. Pour the clam juice into a saucepan and bring it to a boil. Lower the heat and simmer for about 5 minutes, until reduced to about ¼ cup. Set aside to cool.

In a mixing bowl, stir together the clams, oregano, thyme, basil, garlic, hot sauce (if using), and pepper. Stir in the lemon juice. Then stir in the crumbled bacon. Add the breadcrumbs and stir until well combined. Season with salt.

CONTINUED >

Preheat the oven to 500°F (450°F for convection). Brush the par-baked crust with bacon fat and top with the mozzarella cheese. Spoon the clam and bacon mixture over the cheese.

Bake on the middle shelf of the oven for 6 minutes. Then rotate the pan 180 degrees and continue baking 5 to 6 minutes longer, or until the crust turns golden brown, the cheese melts, and the clams and bacon begin to crisp and brown.

Transfer the baked pizza to the stovetop or to a heatproof counter and let cool for 10 minutes. Using an offset spatula or bench blade, carefully slide it around the edge, between the crust and the side of the pan, and then lift the pizza out of the pan and slide it onto a cutting board. Drizzle the pizza with the reduced clam juice and sprinkle with the Parmesan cheese. Garnish with the parsley. Let cool for 2 minutes, then cut into 3- or 4-inch squares and serve.

PUTTANESCA

Puttanesca has a storied history as the pasta of the red-light district. There are a number of stories regarding the origin of this dish, most of them anecdotal, but the common thread is that the sauce is made with capers, garlic, red pepper flakes, olives, anchovies, and pretty much anything else the cooks want to throw in or use up. One theory, which makes sense to me, is that the powerfully fragrant aroma of this sauce emanating from the brothels was very effective at drawing in customers. Of course, it's just a theory, but what is a fact is how delicious this sauce tastes, whether over pasta or on a pizza. Anchovies are often identified with puttanesca, but there is no rule requiring you to use them if you are not a fan. If you are concerned about the anchovies dominating, you can always cut back to only one or two fillets or simply leave them out. For those of us who like anchovies, though, it's that assertive salty, fishy flavor that we really like. If you come to my house, expect to see them used in abundance.

32 ounces (907 g) of any Master Dough (pages 27–35)

1½ cups Crushed Tomato Pizza Sauce (page 46) or All-Purpose Marinara Pizza Sauce (page 49)

½ cup pitted green (Spanish) olives, quartered

¼ cup capers

1 tablespoon caper juice

½ teaspoon red pepper flakes (optional)

2 to 8 salted anchovies, finely chopped

Zest of 1 lemon

2 tablespoons olive oil

8 garlic cloves, chopped

2 cups grated mozzarella, provolone, or fontina cheese (or a combination)

½ cup sliced Genoa (or other) salami, cut into 1-inch-long, ¼-inch wide strips

¼ cup freshly grated Parmesan, Romano, or Asiago cheese

1 teaspoon fresh oregano, or ¼ teaspoon dried oregano

¼ cup chopped Italian parsley or chopped basil

Follow the instructions for panning and par-baking Sicilian-style dough (see page 139).

While the dough is rising, make the sauce for the puttanesca: Pour the pizza sauce into a bowl. Add the olives, capers, caper juice, pepper flakes, anchovies, and lemon zest and stir to combine. Heat the oil in a small skillet over medium heat. When the oil is hot, add the garlic and sauté for 3 seconds, then immediately stir the garlic and the oil into the sauce.

CONTINUED >

Preheat the oven to 500°F (450°F for convection). Ladle the sauce over the par-baked crust. Top with the mozzarella and then cover the cheese with the salami strips.

Bake on the middle shelf of the oven for 6 minutes. Then rotate the pan 180 degrees and bake 5 to 7 minutes longer, or until the crust turns golden brown and the cheese begins to bubble and caramelize.

Transfer the baked pizza to the stovetop or to a heatproof counter and let cool for 2 minutes. Using an offset spatula or bench blade, carefully slide it around the edge, between the crust and the side of the pan, and then lift the pizza out of the pan and slide it onto a cutting board. Garnish with the grated Parmesan, oregano, and parsley. Cut into 3- or 4-inch squares and serve.

"GREEK"

I believe a good case can be made to prove that pizza, as we know it, probably originated in Greece before migrating to Naples on its way to conquering the world. Fifteen years ago, when I taught at the Providence campus of Johnson & Wales University, my wife and I used to eat regularly at a restaurant in Warwick, Rhode Island, called Campanella's. My favorite dish on their menu was what they called their Greek spinach pizza, which consisted of a bed of spinach, on top of melted pizza cheese, with a Greek salad added on top of that just before folding it like a gyro and serving it. The vinaigrette on the salad tied all the flavors together in a very enjoyable way! It's been many years since I ate at Campanella's, but it is the indelible memory of those flavors that inspired this updated version, served on a Sicilian-style dough instead of Campanella's soft foldable crust. In my mind, it's just a short jaunt from Greece to Naples to Sicily, so this pizza is my attempt to evoke all three cultures (so similar yet so distinct) in a pizza that serves as a complete meal and journey unto itself.

NOTES: *If your feta cheese doesn't come with brine, simply blend an additional 2 tablespoons of crumbled feta cheese in its place.*

Baby arugula, as well as baby spinach and kale, can be found at most supermarkets in 5-ounce plastic containers, usually in the organic section. It looks like a lot for one pizza, but it shrinks down considerably when cooked.

32 ounces (907 g) of any Master Dough (pages 27–35)

5 ounces baby greens (arugula, spinach, or kale)

4 tablespoons olive oil

8 garlic cloves, finely chopped or pressed

½ cup pitted and quartered kalamata olives

2 tablespoons freshly squeezed lemon juice

2 tablespoons feta brine

2 tablespoons red wine vinegar

1½ cups cherry tomatoes or grape tomatoes, halved

1½ cups grated kasseri, provolone, fontina, or mozzarella cheese

¼ teaspoon kosher salt

Pinch of freshly ground black pepper

1 cup crumbled feta cheese

4 ounces fresh goat cheese

¼ cup chopped flat-leaf parsley (optional)

CONTINUED >

"GREEK," CONTINUED >

Follow the instructions for panning and par-baking Sicilian-style dough (see page 139).

While the dough is rising, wash and drain the baby greens to remove any grit. Heat the olive oil in a large sauté pan or pot over high heat. When the oil is hot, add the greens and garlic and stir until the greens are coated with the oil. Lower the heat to medium, add the kalamata olives and lemon juice, and cover the pan with a lid for 30 to 60 seconds to steam the greens without overcooking it (it should remain bright green and just slightly wilted but not limp). Remove the lid, strain the pan juice into a small bowl, and transfer the greens mixture to a separate bowl to cool. Return the pan juice to the pan and cook for about 2 minutes over medium-high heat, or until reduced by half. Add the feta brine and the vinegar, then pour the mixture over the greens. Season with the salt and pepper, and toss until combined.

Preheat the oven to 500°F (450°F for convection). Spread the greens over the par-baked pizza crust. Top with the cherry tomatoes, then sprinkle the kasseri cheese over the greens and tomatoes.

Bake on the middle shelf of the oven for 6 minutes. Then rotate the pan 180 degrees and bake 5 to 7 minutes longer, or until the crust turns golden brown and the cheese begins to caramelize. Remove the pan from the oven and top with the feta and goat cheese. Return the pan to the oven for 2 minutes to lightly melt the cheese.

Transfer the baked pizza to the stovetop or to a heatproof counter and let cool for 2 minutes. Using an offset spatula or bench blade, carefully slide it around the edge, between the crust and the side of the pan, and then lift the pizza out of the pan and slide it onto a cutting board. Garnish with the parsley, if using, then cut into 3- or 4-inch squares and serve.

ROMAN-STYLE PIZZAS

This is the category that I think has the potential to grow faster around the world than any other. A relative newcomer to the American scene known to us as Roman-style pizza and better known in Italy as pizza *al taglio* ("pizza baked in a pan"), it is traditionally a simple, long, white (Bianca) or red (Rossa) flatbread lopped off into portions and sold by weight. In some ways this style is like thin focaccia and could even be called that if we didn't now associate this recent iteration with Rome instead of Genoa, where focaccia is king. As with every pizza, there is no definitive method or version, but there are two prototypes in particular that represent the currently most popular approaches. I am referring specifically to two of the more inventive versions of recent times: the thicker-crusted Gabrielle Bonci version (see Resources, page 175) and the thinner-, wetter-dough approach of Massimiliano Saieva, both of which bring together the best elements of the "dough with something on it" model in a new and distinctive presentation. For my version, I have borrowed from each of these two master pizzaiolos: it is not as wet as nor is it fermented for as long as the Saieva method (up to 92 hours), but it is wetter and thinner crusted than the Bonci method. It has a crust that is only ½ inch high, a feature that differentiates it from the other styles in this book. Therefore, we will be putting less dough (28 ounces/794 g) in the pans for these pizzas than for the other styles. I believe that my method is easier to make in a home kitchen, and it doesn't require long hours of practice. However, it does require patience and some practice, but after you've made it once or twice, you will quickly absorb the ins and outs of this method and be able to make it as easily as the deep-pan and focaccia styles.

Note: One of the trademarks of pizzerias serving Roman-style pizza is that they cut the squares using a large pair of kitchen scissors instead of a knife. If you have a good pair of such scissors, you will find that using them to portion out the pizza is fun and easy. However, you can also use a large chef's knife. If you'd like to purchase a pair of the specialty scissors used by the professionals, look in the Resources section on page 175 for the link to the Roman Pizza Academy.

THE CLASSICS: ROSSA (RED) AND BIANCA (WHITE)

MAKES ONE 12 BY 17-INCH ROMAN-STYLE PIZZA

In the style of Rome's famous Antico Forno Campo de' Fiori, these are my own versions of the red and white classics that people line up for all day long. The Rossa and Bianca focaccias (page 125) and my Roman versions are similar, but these have a thinner, lighter crust. Of course, at Antico Forno they make theirs about 7 feet long, so this adaptation is designed to deliver the same joy, in your own kitchen, without having to travel all the way to Rome. As you will see, what makes these pizzas memorable is how amazing this dough tastes when it's properly fermented and hydrated, and then baked in a hot oven, even a home oven. The simplicity of the toppings, either red or white, not only add their own distinctiveness, but also, and more important, they allow the complex and deeply satisfying flavor of the crust to take center stage.

5 tablespoons plus 3 teaspoons olive oil, plus more for dimpling

28 ounces (794 g) of any Master Dough (pages 27–35)

1½ cups Crushed Tomato Pizza Sauce (page 46) or All-Purpose Marinara Pizza Sauce (page 49; for the Rossa only)

½ cup Herb Oil (page 54) or olive oil (for the Bianca)

1 teaspoon fresh oregano, or ¼ teaspoon dried oregano (for the Rossa)

Coarse sea salt or kosher salt, as needed (for the Bianca)

At least 4 hours before you plan to bake the pizza, line a 12 by 17-inch sheet pan with parchment paper or a silicone baking mat, and then oil the pan, including the interior sides, with 3 tablespoons of olive oil. Begin panning and dimpling the dough, at 20-minute intervals, as shown on page 13. After three to four rounds of dimpling and resting, the dough will have relaxed enough to cover the whole pan. At this point, coat the dough with 2 teaspoons of the olive oil, cover the pan loosely with plastic wrap, and let the dough rise at room temperature for 3 hours. The dough will rise slightly below the rim of the pan.

Twenty minutes before baking the pizza, preheat the oven to 500°F (450°F for convection). If making the Rossa pizza, dip your fingers in some olive oil and gently dimple the dough just before baking it—you will spread the sauce over the dough after a 5-minute pre-bake. If making the Bianca pizza, ladle or drizzle the Herb Oil or olive oil over the dough and spread it gently with your fingertips to evenly cover it without degassing the dough.

CONTINUED >

Bake the pizza on the middle shelf of the oven for 5 minutes. If making the Rossa, remove it from the oven and ladle the red sauce over the surface, spreading it with the back of the ladle or a rubber spatula. In either instance, rotate the pan 180 degrees and continue baking 6 to 9 minutes longer, or until both the top and the undercrust are golden brown (the Rossa will take a few minutes longer than the Bianca).

Transfer the baked pizza to the stovetop or to a heatproof counter and let cool for 2 minutes. Using an offset spatula or bench blade, carefully slide it around the edge, between the crust and the side of the pan, and then lift the pizza out of the pan and slide it onto a cutting board. For the Rossa pizza, sprinkle the crust with the dried oregano; for the Bianca, brush the top with a teaspoon of olive or herb oil and sprinkle it with a small amount of coarse salt and the fresh oregano. Let cool for 2 minutes, then cut with a pair of kitchen scissors or a knife and serve.

GRAPE TOMATO AND RICOTTA CREAM

MAKES ONE 12 BY 17-INCH ROMAN-STYLE PIZZA

One of the charming qualities of many Roman-style pizzas is that they can be topped after they come out of the oven and can be served both hot or cold. They not only taste fresh, like a crisp garden salad, but with their bright, verdant colors, they also are pleasing to the eye. This pizza takes advantage of the refreshing flavor contrast created by the cooked tomatoes and melted cheese and the topping of freshly dressed greens and soft ricotta cream. The dressed greens and cream provide a pleasant counterpoint to the cooked ingredients, and as noted throughout, all of this flavor and textural contrast is just a bonus when it comes with a memorable crust. I think these qualities—the freshness, the bursts of flavor, and the lightness of the crust—are why Roman-style pizzas are going to increase in popularity over the next few years.

NOTE: *The ricotta cream is extremely easy to make. It can be made in advance and used as a garnish on all your salads and vegetable dishes. Imagine it on baked potatoes. Amazing!*

5 tablespoons plus 2 teaspoon olive oil

28 ounces (794 g) of any Master Dough (pages 27–35)

1½ cups coarsely chopped baby arugula or baby kale

1 tablespoon freshly squeezed lemon juice

1 tablespoon balsamic vinegar

¼ teaspoon kosher salt

Pinch of freshly ground black pepper

1½ cups freshly grated mozzarella, provolone, or fontina cheese

1½ cups grape tomatoes or cherry tomatoes, halved

1½ cups Ricotta Cream (page 162)

½ cup freshly grated Parmesan, Romano, or Asiago cheese

At least 4 hours before you plan to bake the pizza, line a 12 by 17-inch sheet pan with parchment paper or a silicone baking mat, and then oil the pan, including the interior sides, with 3 tablespoons of olive oil. Begin panning and dimpling the dough, at 20-minute intervals, as shown on page 13. After three to four rounds of dimpling and resting, the dough will have relaxed enough to cover the whole pan. At this point, coat the dough with 2 teaspoons of the olive oil, cover the pan loosely with plastic wrap, and let the dough rise at room temperature for 3 hours. The dough will rise to slightly below the rim of the pan.

CONTINUED >

While the dough is rising, toss the baby arugula with the remaining 2 table-spoons olive oil, the lemon juice, balsamic vinegar, salt, and pepper. Cover and refrigerate until needed.

Twenty minutes before the pizza is ready to bake, preheat the oven to 500°F (450°F for convection). Top the dough with the grated mozzarella and cover the cheese with a single layer of tomatoes.

Bake the pizza on the middle shelf of the oven for 7 minutes. Then rotate the pan and continue baking 6 to 8 minutes longer, or until the top and the undercrust are both golden brown, the cheese is melted, and bubbly, and the tomatoes are slightly charred.

Transfer the baked pizza to the stovetop or to a heatproof counter and let cool for 2 minutes. Using an offset spatula or bench blade, carefully slide it around the edge, between the crust and the side of the pan, and then lift the pizza out of the pan and slide it onto a cutting board. Cover the baked pizza with the dressed arugula and then top the greens with dollops of the Ricotta Cream. Sprinkle with the grated Parmesan or other dried cheese. Allow 2 minutes for the greens to slightly wilt and the ricotta cream to warm. Then cut with kitchen scissors or a knife and serve.

RICOTTA CREAM

MAKES 1½ CUPS

1 cup whole-milk ricotta cheese

½ cup mascarpone cheese, sour cream, or heavy whipping cream

1 tablespoon sugar

¼ teaspoon salt, plus more as needed

Pinch of freshly ground black pepper, plus more as needed

Combine the ricotta, mascarpone, sugar, salt, and pepper in a mixing bowl and whisk together vigorously for 3 to 5 minutes, until the mixture is smooth and thickened. Taste and add more salt and pepper, if desired. (Note: You can also blend the ingredients in a food processor fitted with the metal blade until thickened and smooth.) This cream will keep in a covered container for at least 7 days in the refrigerator.

SUSAN'S ROSEMARY-GARLIC POTATOES

MAKES ONE 12 BY 17-INCH ROMAN-STYLE PIZZA

This pizza was inspired by an oven-roasted, crispy side dish perfected by my wife, Susan. Her rosemary-garlic potato wedges have become one of the most requested sides whenever we have company for dinner. She usually serves them as an accompaniment with roast chicken or steaks, but I started playing with the recipe (when she wasn't looking) and adapted her potatoes for this Roman-style pizza, which turned out to be quite beautiful and tasty. The prosciutto shreds are, of course, optional and can be omitted for a vegetarian version. The shredded baby kale garnish makes everything pop. But the potatoes are the real stars, and once you've learned how to make them, you can serve them many ways, with or without the pizza.

If you can't find prosciutto or you aren't fond of it, you can substitute other meats such as pancetta, Genoa salami, or crumbled bacon. Regardless, meat is optional. If you are not using meat, add ½ cup freshly grated Parmesan cheese.

I usually add the prosciutto as an uncooked garnish after the pizza is baked, but you can add it to the top of the pizza at the same time as you add the potatoes, so that the threads crisp up in the oven, like bacon. Both versions are wonderful.

9 tablespoons plus 2 teaspoons olive oil

28 ounces (794 g) of any Master Dough (pages 27–35)

2 pounds waxy potatoes (such as Yukon Gold, Red Bliss, Blue, or a combination)

8 garlic cloves, peeled and coarsely chopped

1 fresh rosemary sprig

¼ teaspoon kosher salt, plus more as needed

Freshly ground black pepper

2 cups baby kale or other baby greens

1½ cups grape tomatoes or cherry tomatoes, halved

1 tablespoon freshly squeezed lemon juice

1 tablespoon balsamic vinegar

1½ cups freshly grated mozzarella, provolone, or fontina cheese

3 ounces thinly sliced prosciutto, cut into 2-inch matchsticks, or ½ cup freshly grated Parmesan cheese

At least 4 hours before you plan to bake the pizza, line a 12 by 17-inch sheet pan with parchment paper or a silicone baking mat, and then oil the pan, including the interior sides, with 3 tablespoons of olive oil. Begin panning and dimpling the dough, at 20-minute intervals, as shown on page 13. After three to four rounds of dimpling and resting, the dough will have relaxed enough to cover the whole pan. At this point, coat the dough with 2 teaspoons of the olive oil, cover the pan loosely with plastic wrap, and let the dough rise at room temperature for 3 hours.

CONTINUED >

The dough will rise to slightly below the rim of the pan.

While the dough is rising, prepare the potatoes. Preheat the oven to 425°F (with or without convection). Grease a sheet pan or baking dish with 1 tablespoon of olive oil and set aside. If you are using baby potatoes, wash but don't peel them and cut each one in half. If you are using larger potatoes, cut them into 4 to 8 wedges. Place the potatoes in a bowl and add the garlic. Scrape the rosemary needles off the stem and add them to the bowl. Add the salt, a pinch of pepper, and 3 tablespoons of the oil. Using a rubber spatula, stir all the ingredients until the potatoes are evenly coated with the oil and seasonings. Transfer the mixture to the prepared sheet pan or baking dish and spread in an even layer. Roast on the middle shelf of the oven for 20 minutes. Remove the pan from the oven and use a rubber or plastic spatula to get underneath and stir the potatoes, flipping over as many of them as you can to expose their uncooked side. Return the pan to the oven for another 20 minutes. Remove the pan from the oven and repeat the stirring and flipping. Again, return them to the oven for another 20 minutes and repeat this procedure every 20 minutes until the potatoes turn golden brown and become crisp, about an hour to an hour and a half. Immediately remove the pan from the oven and set it aside to cool.

In a large bowl, toss the baby kale and the tomatoes with the remaining 2 tablespoons of oil, the lemon juice, and balsamic vinegar. Add salt and a pinch of pepper, if desired. Cover the bowl with plastic wrap and refrigerate until you are ready to assemble the pizza.

Twenty minutes before the pizza is ready to bake, preheat the oven to 500°F (450°F for convection). Top the dough with the grated mozzarella (or other) cheese.

Bake on the middle shelf of the oven for 6 minutes. Remove the pan from the oven and top the pizza with a layer of the potato mixture. Then rotate the pan 180 degrees and bake 6 to 10 minutes longer, or until the potatoes recrisp and the top and the undercrust are both golden brown.

Transfer the baked pizza to the stovetop or to a heatproof counter and let cool for 2 minutes. Using an offset spatula or bench blade, carefully slide it around the edge, between the crust and the side of the pan, and then lift the pizza out of the pan and slide it onto a cutting board. Using a slotted spoon, spread the dressed kale and tomato mixture over the baked pizza, then top with the prosciutto (or Parmesan cheese, if not using any meat). Allow 2 to 3 minutes for the greens to slightly wilt, then cut into 3- or 4-inch squares and serve.

NDUJA CIOPPINO

Brad English, producer and cofounder of Pizza Quest, and I came up with this pizza for the 2016 Forno Bravo Oven Expo, where we were given a big packet of La Quercia *nduja*, a product that I'd never used before. When I added it to the seafood mixture, I realized that I had discovered a powerful tool for my flavor arsenal. What is *nduja*? Well, I've seen it described in a variety of ways. Generically, it's a Calabrian salami paste, which, according to Calabrian tradition, can be made with nearly every part of the pig. La Quercia, however, makes theirs by grinding up prosciutto and speck (smoked prosciutto), mixing it with chile peppers and salt, and then curing it for 9 to 12 months. They refer to it on their website as a "spicy prosciutto spread," but that doesn't come close to describing how amazing it is.

This Nduja Cioppino will work with any version or brand of *nduja*. However, I prefer the La Quercia product, not just because it's domestically made and easy to order but also because it is made with only antibiotic-free pork. You should track some down (see Resources, page 175, for website information) and make this pizza, which is, essentially, a spicy seafood stew served on a delicious Roman-style pizza crust. Once you taste it, you'll be glad you went to the trouble.

7 tablespoons plus 2 teaspoons olive oil	1 pound mussels, in the shell	2 tablespoons Herb Oil (page 54) or olive oil
28 ounces (794 g) of any Master Dough (pages 27–35)	8 ounces large or medium shrimp, shelled and deveined	1½ cups whole grape tomatoes or cherry tomatoes, cut into halves or quarters, depending on size
8 garlic cloves, coarsely chopped	1 cup dry white wine, such as sauvignon blanc	
1 large red or green bell pepper, or 2 Anaheim, Fresno, or jalapeño peppers, seeded and cut into 1-inch strips	8 ounces *nduja*, cut into 1-inch pieces	1 cup freshly grated Parmesan, Romano, or Asiago cheese
	¼ cup freshly squeezed lemon juice	½ cup chopped flat-leaf parsley

At least 4 hours before you plan to bake the pizza, line a 12 by 17-inch sheet pan with parchment paper or a silicone baking mat, and then oil the pan, including the interior sides, with 3 tablespoons of olive oil. Begin panning and dimpling the dough, at 20-minute intervals, as shown on page 13. After three to four rounds of dimpling and resting, the dough will have relaxed enough to cover the whole

CONTINUED >

pan. At this point, coat the dough with 2 teaspoons of the olive oil, cover the pan loosely with plastic wrap, and let the dough rise at room temperature for 3 hours. The dough will rise to slightly below the rim of the pan.

While the dough is rising, preheat the oven to 500°F (475°F for convection). Meanwhile, in a Dutch oven or other ovenproof baking pot with a lid, heat 2 tablespoons of the olive oil over medium-high heat. Add the garlic and peppers, give them a quick stir, and then immediately add the mussels and shrimp. Remove the pan from the heat, add the white wine, and cover with the lid. Transfer to the oven and roast for 8 to 10 minutes, or until the mussels open and the shrimp have turned red. Remove the pan from the oven, add the *nduja* and lemon juice, and stir. Strain the juice from the seafood-*nduja* mixture. Transfer the seafood-*nduja* mixture to a bowl and set aside to cool. If desired, remove the mussels from their shells. Return the juice to the pot, bring to a boil over high heat, and boil for 3 to 5 minutes, until the juice is reduced to a syruplike consistency. Set aside.

Twenty minutes before you are ready to bake the pizza, preheat the oven to 500°F (450°F for convection). Drizzle 2 tablespoons of the Herb Oil over the pizza dough and spread it with your fingertips to cover the surface, gently dimpling the dough to help spread the oil but not enough to degas the dough.

Bake on the middle shelf of the oven for 7 minutes. Remove the pan from the oven, spoon the seafood-*nduja* mixture over the dough, and cover with the tomatoes. Then rotate the pan 180 degrees and bake 6 to 10 minutes longer, or until the top crust and undercrust are both golden brown.

Transfer the baked pizza to the stovetop or to a heatproof counter and let cool for 10 minutes. Using an offset spatula or bench blade, carefully slide it around the edge, between the crust and the side of the pan, and then lift the pizza out of the pan and slide it onto a cutting board. Drizzle the reduced seafood-*nduja* juice over the pizza and sprinkle with the Parmesan cheese. Garnish with the parsley. Let cool for 2 minutes, then cut into 3- or 4-inch squares and serve.

SWEET ONION-BÉCHAMEL WITH MORTADELLA

MAKES ONE 12 BY 17-INCH ROMAN-STYLE PIZZA

White pizzas are an essential subcategory of the pizza canon, and there are many ways to make them. First (and most obvious), don't use tomato sauce, though it's okay to garnish the pizza with some fresh tomatoes. Second, add ricotta cheese to the mix. Ricotta is often the workhorse of white pizzas, such as the classic New York–style white spinach slice, because it's pleasantly subtle, plays well with companion toppings, and doesn't melt into a greasy, gooey, stringy mess. However, white pizza does not require ricotta, even though it's a wonderful option.

Another way to make a white pizza, like the one we are about to make here, is to replace the tomato sauce with a white sauce. Yes, I'm talking about a béchamel sauce, the inimitable French "mother sauce," made either with or without cheese. I've made the following white pizza without cheese, and it's not bad. But, like a lasagna that's often made with both béchamel sauce and cheese, it's even more amazing with cheese. This pizza also calls for our signature Carmelized Balsamic Onion Marmalade, which can be made ahead. In a pinch, you could just use regular sautéed, caramelized onions.

One of the atypical toppings for this white pizza is mortadella, the mild, soft, northern Italian salumi that many Americans know as bologna but pronounce as "baloney." There is a lot of inexpensive bologna available, but I urge you to hold out for its higher-quality antecedent: mortadella. You'll be glad you did.

This version also calls for soft, only slightly warmed mortadella, which is added just before the pizza goes back into the oven for a brief final bake. However, if you like the taste and texture of fried baloney, as I do, you can add the mortadella halfway through the bake, when you rotate the pan at the 6-minute mark.

4 tablespoons olive oil

28 ounces (794 g) of any Master Dough (pages 27–35)

BÉCHAMEL

1½ cups whole milk

4 tablespoons unsalted butter

2 tablespoons all-purpose or bread flour

¼ teaspoon kosher salt

Pinch of freshly ground black pepper

Pinch of freshly grated nutmeg

1 large red bell pepper, cut into ½-inch pieces

1½ cups grated melting cheese (such as provolone, fontina, Gruyère, or Cheddar)

1½ cups Carmelized Balsamic Onion Marmalade (page 56)

4 ounces thinly sliced mortadella or other mild deli meat, cut into 1½-inch-long matchsticks

¼ cup finely chopped flat-leaf parsley

At least 4 hours before you plan to bake the pizza, line a 12 by 17-inch sheet pan with parchment paper or a silicone baking mat, and then oil the pan, including the interior sides, with 3 tablespoons of olive oil. Begin panning and dimpling the dough, at 20-minute intervals, as shown on page 13. After three to four rounds of dimpling and resting, the dough will have relaxed enough to cover the whole pan. At this point, coat the dough with 2 teaspoons of the olive oil, cover the pan loosely with plastic wrap, and let the dough rise at room temperature for 3 hours. The dough will rise to slightly below the rim of the pan.

While the dough is rising, make the béchamel. In a small saucepan, heat the milk over medium-low heat until just warm, and set it aside. In a separate saucepan, melt the butter over medium heat. Whisk in the flour to make a smooth paste and cook for about 60 seconds to cook out the starchy flavor but not to brown it. Slowly whisk in the warmed milk, then bring the sauce to a simmer, stirring gently with a wooden spoon. When the sauce thickens enough to coat the back of the spoon, remove it from the heat, add the salt, pepper, and nutmeg, and set it aside to cool.

Heat the remaining 1 tablespoon of oil in a frying pan over medium-high heat. When the oil is hot, add the bell pepper and sauté for about 2 minutes, or until shiny but not limp. Remove the pan from the heat and set it aside to cool.

Preheat the oven to 500°F (450°F for convection). Just before baking the pizza, stir the grated cheese into the cooled béchamel sauce and ladle the sauce over the dough. Spoon the marmalade over the sauce and sprinkle with the bell pepper.

Bake the pizza on the middle shelf of the oven for 6 minutes. Rotate the pan 180 degrees and continue baking 6 to 10 minutes longer, or until the top crust and undercrust are both golden brown and the onions have begun to char slightly. Remove the pizza from the oven and sprinkle the mortadella over the onions. Return the pizza to the oven for 2 to 3 minutes to warm up the meat but not to fully crisp it.

Transfer the baked pizza to the stovetop or to a heatproof counter and let cool for 10 minutes. Using an offset spatula or bench blade, carefully slide it around the edge, between the crust and the side of the pan, and then lift the pizza out of the pan and slide it onto a cutting board. Garnish with the parsley. Let cool for about 2 minutes, then cut into 3- or 4-inch squares and serve.

AVOCADO "SCAMPI"

MAKES ONE 12 BY 17-INCH ROMAN-STYLE PIZZA

I call this pizza a scampi—a term usually associated with shrimp or langoustines that have been cooked in a lemon, butter, and garlic sauce—mainly because it delivers the scampi "experience" but with avocado slices instead of shrimp. Could you make it with shrimp? Of course! After all, shrimp scampi is a very popular classic dish, but this version is a vegetarian-friendly alternative that tastes just as wonderful as it would if it were made with shrimp. The scampi sauce that is drizzled over the top just before serving is a variation of a lemon-garlic aioli inspired by the famous shrimp scampi I greedily consumed at San Francisco's legendary Caffe Sport. Their version was made with jumbo Gulf prawns drenched in lemon-garlic sauce and served with delicious sautéed zucchini spears. The first time I had it there, I was twenty-seven years old, and it left such an indelible taste memory that I couldn't wait to reinterpret it as a pizza. I haven't been back to Caffe Sport in many years, but when I recently checked their website, I saw that Scampi al Antonio is still on the menu, so a revisit is definitely on my bucket list. Until then, I will happily enjoy the spirit of Scampi al Antonio, whether it is made with shrimp or, in this new Roman-style pizza version, with avocado.

3 tablespoons plus 2 teaspoons olive oil

28 ounces (794 g) of any Master Dough (pages 27–35)

1½ cups grated fontina, mozzarella, provolone, or Taleggio cheese

6 Roma or plum tomatoes, cut crosswise into ¼-inch-thick slices

2 large or 3 medium-size ripe avocados

1 cup aioli (page 174)

¼ cup chopped flat-leaf parsley or cilantro

At least 4 hours before you plan to bake the pizza, line a 12 by 17-inch sheet pan with parchment paper or a silicone baking mat, and then oil the pan, including the interior sides, with 3 tablespoons of olive oil. Begin panning and dimpling the dough, at 20-minute intervals, as shown on page 13. After three to four rounds of dimpling and resting, the dough will have relaxed enough to cover the whole pan. At this point, coat the dough with 2 teaspoons of the olive oil, cover the pan loosely with plastic wrap, and let the dough rise at room temperature for 3 hours. The dough will rise to slightly below the rim of the pan.

CONTINUED >

Twenty minutes before baking the pizza, preheat the oven to 500°F (450°F for convection). Cover the surface of the dough with the grated cheese.

Bake on the middle shelf of the oven for 6 minutes. Remove the pan from the oven and cover the cheese with the sliced tomatoes. Then rotate the pan 180 degrees and continue baking 8 to 10 minutes longer, or until the cheese is melted and bubbly and the top crust and undercrust are both golden brown.

While the pizza is baking, cut and split the avocados in half, remove and discard the pits, and use a tablespoon to scoop out each avocado half in one piece. Place the halves on a cutting board and cut the avocados into ¼-inch-thick wedges.

Transfer the baked pizza to the stovetop or to a heatproof counter and let cool for 2 minutes. Using an offset spatula or bench blade, carefully slide it around the edge, between the crust and the side of the pan, and then lift the pizza out of the pan and slide it onto a cutting board. Top the pizza with the avocado wedges and drizzle them with the aioli sauce. Garnish with the parsley or cilantro, then cut into 3- to 4-inch squares and serve.

AIOLI
MAKES 1 CUP

1 egg	¼ teaspoon kosher salt, plus more as needed	½ cup olive oil, plus more as needed
3 egg yolks		
2 garlic cloves, grated or minced	4 tablespoons freshly squeezed lemon juice (from 1 lemon)	Pinch of freshly ground black pepper or cayenne pepper
½ teaspoon Dijon mustard		

In a blender (or whisk by hand in a bowl), whiz together the egg, egg yolks, garlic, mustard, salt, and 1 tablespoon of the lemon juice. On slow speed, slowly drizzle in the oil. As you add the oil, the sauce will thicken to the consistency of mayonnaise (if it thickens too much, add more oil). Transfer the sauce to a bowl and whisk in the remaining 3 tablespoons of lemon juice and season with salt and pepper (or cayenne), if desired. Cover and refrigerate for up to 5 days.

RESOURCES

This list is by no means comprehensive, but will provide enough information to get you up and running or lead you to additional sources with more detailed information. Given the power of the internet, you can easily track down what you need using a keyword search, but the following represents my recommendations.

BOOKS, MAGAZINES, AND OTHER PIZZA MEDIA

There are so many good pizza books to choose from, but the following are all useful and loaded with excellent recipe ideas for all styles, including pan pizzas:

- *American Pie: My Search for the Perfect Pizza*, Peter Reinhart
- *Bianco: Pizza, Pasta and Other Foods I Like*, Chris Bianco
- *Mastering Pizza*, Marc Vetri and David Joachim
- *My Pizza*, Jim Lahey
- *Pizza*, Gabrielle Bonci
- *Pizza: A Slice of Heaven*, Ed Levine
- *Pizza Camp*, Joe Beddia
- *The Elements of Pizza*, Ken Forkish
- *The Pizza Bible*, Tony Gemignani
- *The United States of Pizza*, Craig Priebe and Diane Jacob
- *Where to Eat Pizza*, Daniel Young

There are currently two professional magazines that are free to anyone in the trade (or with enough passion to sound like you're in the trade). *Pizza Today* (pizzatoday.com) and *PMQ* (pmq.com). Both provide e-newsletters and digital versions as well as printed magazines, and include recipes, personality profiles, interviews, and business tips as well as news regarding upcoming pizza conventions, expos, and trade shows.

Other useful websites and media: There are too many to list and there are more every day, so do an internet search if you want to immerse yourself. But, here are a few links to get you started.

- Pizza Quest (fornobravo.com/ pizzaquest) is my own pizza website, filled with interviews, video webisodes, recipes, and guest columns, all in pursuit of the perfect pizza and to celebrate artisanship wherever we find it. The videos, in longer episode format, are also featured on mybluprint.com.
- *The Pizza Show*, with Frank Pinello, ViceTV (video.vice.com/ en_us/show/pizza-show).
- *The Brooklyn Pizza Crew* (brooklynpizzacrew.com).
- Roman Pizza Academy videos of Massimiliano Saieva (search for these on YouTube, and they will also lead to videos of many other Roman-style video masters).
- And, finally, the pizza episode of David Chang's Netflix show *Ugly Delicious*.

SOURCING

Cheese

Everyone has their preferred cheese brands and many types will work with the recipes in this book. That said, for Wisconsin brick cheese, which is hard to find in most supermarket cheese sections, you can refer to the following websites for more on the history and methodology as well as where to track down this unique, relatively unknown cheese:

- Klondike Cheese: klondikecheese.com
- Widmer's Cheese: widmerscheese.com/ the-story-of-wisconsin-brick-cheese
- Zimmerman Cheese: wisconsincheese.com/ wi-cheese-companies/36/ zimmerman-cheese-inc

- For Italian-style cheeses, again, there are many excellent brands to choose from, both domestic and imported. But for a one stop site, full of thumbnail descriptions as well as superb cheeses of many types, I suggest BelGioioso Cheese: belgioioso.com/Products

Flour

The pizza dough formulas in this book were designed to be made with bread flour that has a protein content of approximately 12.5 percent. Some brands of all-purpose flour, such as King Arthur, have nearly that amount of protein (approximately 11.7 percent) and are acceptable substitutes. I do not promote one brand over another except to say that all of the major American bread flour brands will work in these recipes. These brands include Central Milling (also packaged for Whole Foods as their 365 Brand), General Mills (such as Better for Bread and also Harvest King), King Arthur, and many locally milled flours produced in small batches. In the UK, Europe, Australia, and Asia most of these brands are not available so, unless you can find equivalent local brands, another option is to buy flour directly from your favorite bakeries or pizzerias. As long

as they know you will not be opening a competing business they are likely to be willing to help you out.

The recipes in this book will also work with whole grain and sprouted flours, such as any supermarket brand of whole wheat or whole rye flour; but they are especially suited to work with flour made from sprouted wheat. There are currently only a few brands producing and distributing this type of flour (Ardent Mills, Arrowhead Mills, Bay State Milling, Essential Eating, King Arthur, One Degree, and To Your Health, in addition to a number of small, regional companies). For more general information on sprouted grain flours, try these links:

- healthyflour.com/ (To Your Health Sprouted Flour Co.)
- lindleymills.com/super-sprout/super-sprout-faq-s.html (Lindley Mills)
- onegreenplanet.org/vegan-health/flour-power-10-reasons-you-should-bake-with-sprouted-whole-grain-flour
- essentialeating.com

Meats

Many of the recipes in this book call for various types of salumi, charcuterie, sausage, and

specialty deli meat products. As with cheese, there are many fine brands, and most supermarkets and gourmet food stores carry quality meats. However, here are some links to companies whose products I have used with great success. Their sites also contain excellent product information:

- Creminelli Fine Meats: creminelli.com
- LaQuercia: laquercia.us
- Nduja Artisans Salumeria: ndujaartisans.com
- Nueske's: nueskes.com/about

Pans and Tools

The pizzas in this book can be made without specialty or hard-to-find equipment. But many of you will want to track down the tools that the professionals use, so here are some links to sources:

- Allied Pans: alliedpans.com
- Artisan Pizza Solutions, for all sorts of pizza making tools, including the special scissors for cutting Roman-style pizzas: artisanpizzasolutions.com/pizza-taglio-tools
- Detroit Style Pizza Company: detroitstylepizza.com
- Lloyd Pans (see the photo on page 7, featuring many of their pans): lloydpans.com

SOURDOUGH RESOURCES

We merely scratch the surface of sourdough baking in this book but it is vast category and growing in importance and popularity. Here are some additional resources:

- Sourdough Home offers a full list of recommended books and other resources: sourdoughhome.com/index .php?content=resources

- Northwest Sourdough: northwestsourdough.com

I highly recommend Richard Miscovich's sourdough course available on craftsy.com.

CLASSES

Pizza making classes are becoming increasingly popular and many cooking schools are now offering courses on pan pizza in addition to Neapolitan styles. The following list includes a few of the best professional programs, as well as a free video course taught by me for home cooks.

- Craftsy Video Course on Making Artisan Pizza at Home, with Peter Reinhart: craftsy.com

- North American Pizza and Culinary Academy (Chicago): pizzaculinaryacademy.com

- Pizza School NYC: pizzaschool.com

- The Roman Pizza Academy (Miami): romanpizzaacademy.com

- Tony Gemignani's International School of Pizza (San Francisco): internationalschoolofpizza.com

PIZZERIAS

If you're interested in seeing what other *pizzaioli* are doing with these styles, there are many places to encounter pan pizza in the wild. There are too many to list, but here are some pizzerias doing extraordinary work with pan pizza styles of the type introduced in this book:

Roman-Style
- Alice (Philadelphia)
- Bonci Pizzeria (Chicago)
- Eight & Sand (Charlotte, NC)
- Il Romanista (Los Angeles)
- Pizzarium (Miami, not to be confused with Gabrielle Bonci's Pizzarium in Rome)
- Rione (Philadelphia)
- Rock, Pizza, Scissors (NYC)
- Triple Beam (Los Angeles)

Detroit-Style
- In Detroit: Buddy's Pizza, Cloverleaf Bar and Restaurant, Belle Isle Pizza, Jet's Pizza, Loui's Pizza
- Blue Pan Pizza (Denver, CO)
- Brown Dog Pizza (Telluride, CO)

- Emmy Squared (NYC and Brooklyn)
- Mash'd (Frisco, TX)
- Rock, Pizza, Scissors (NYC)
- Paulie Gee's (Chicago)
- Sofia (NYC)
- Union Squared (Chicago)

WRITE TO ME

I know that many of you will want to share the name of your favorite pizzeria with others and may even wonder why your favorite isn't on this list (as noted, there are just too many, and the above are just examples of the ones I know). I'd be happy to start a guest column on my website with your stories of best places, or anecdotes regarding your own quest for the perfect pizza. Write to me at peter@pizzaquest.com if you'd like to be a contributor.

GLOSSARY

BLUE STEEL PANS The pans that were originally, and to this date, the most associated with Detroit-style pizza as developed by Gus Guerra in 1946. The pans were used in the automotive industry for holding nuts and bolts as well as other tools but, as Gus discovered, they also conduct heat perfectly for achieving the distinctive crackly, buttery Detroit-style crust. There are now many other types of pans that also work to achieve the same quality of crust.

BRICK CHEESE A Wisconsin-made washed-rind cow's milk cheese with excellent melting properties. See box, page 9, for more info.

DETROIT-STYLE PIZZA For our purposes, this is a deep-pan pizza baked in pans with side walls at least 2 inches high in order to trap the melting cheese around the edge to create a crispy cheese "frico." Gus Guerra's original pizzeria, *Buddy's Rendezvous* (which later became *Buddy's Pizza*) is credited as the birthplace of this style, but it is now made in many other famous Detroit pizzerias as well as pizzerias around the country.

DIMPLING A term used to describe a method for spreading dough within its pan through a series of fingertip pressings (dimples) followed by 20- to 30-minute resting periods that allow the gluten to relax enough for additional spreading with each dimpling cycle until the whole surface of the pan is covered. See page 13 for a pictorial description.

DOUGH CARAMELIZATION Caramelization refers to the browning of sugars when the temperature exceeds 325°F. With bread or pizza dough, only the surface of the dough, the crust, is able to get that hot, which is why only the crust turns golden brown. Note: There is a second type of caramelization, caused by partial protein amino acids in combination with natural sugars and high heat, called the Maillard reaction. Because flour contains both sugars and proteins, some of the dough caramelization is due to both sugar and Maillard activity, which lends bread crust its unique color and flavor. This complexity is especially apparent in pizza crust.

DOUGH, COARSE AND SHAGGY TO SMOOTH AND DEVELOPED During the first few minutes of mixing, while the ingredients are still absorbing the liquid (see *Dough Hydration*), and prior to full gluten development, the dough looks pebbly and kind of like a textured rug, thus the term "shaggy." After about five minutes, as the gluten strands begin to organize and weave together, developing into a kind of fabriclike texture, the dough becomes smoother and almost shiny.

DOUGH FORMULA In baking, a formula is even more valued than a recipe, because it expresses the nature of the dough as a ratio between each ingredient and the flour. Once a formula is established, a baker can then make any size batch of dough (the recipe). For example, a typical bread or pizza dough contains 2 percent salt, 0.5 percent to 1 percent instant yeast, and 60 percent to 80 percent water, as well as optional ingredients also expressed in percentages, such as oil, sugar, and even milk, eggs, and spices or herbs. The percentage is determined by dividing the ingredient weight by the total flour weight, then multiplying by 100 (example: 2 g salt divided by 100 g flour = .02. When multiplied by 100 it becomes 2 percent).

DOUGH HYDRATION The percentage of water or other liquid added to the flour determines the firmness or softness of the dough. Typical pizza dough contains 60 percent to 72 percent water to flour, whereas the doughs used in this book are 80 percent water to flour, thus making for a much stickier dough, but one that can expand more in the pan during fermentation and baking, creating large, irregular holes in the crumb structure of the dough.

DOUGH RECIPE As noted previously, the recipe is the specific weight or amount of each ingredient for a specified size batch of dough.

FERMENTATION The activity of yeast, and also bacteria, seeking glucose and other simple sugars upon which to feed and grow is called fermentation. The by-product of this activity is the release of carbon dioxide, ethyl alcohol, and acid (both lactic and acetic). Whether in dough or any food (such as in pickling), fermentation transforms its food source from one thing into something else, causing, in the case of bread, the claylike dough to come to life, during which it grows in size as the developing carbon dioxide, trapped by the dough walls, is similar to blowing up a balloon. The dough also develops flavor from the alcohol and acid development.

FOCACCIA Literally "from the hearth (*foca*)," focaccia is an Italian flatbread associated with the northwest region of Italy called Liguria, whose capital is Genoa. It can be baked in a pan or directly on the hearth and can be round or rectangular. The Genovese style is typically baked throughout the day, with various toppings, in a rectangular pan, then cut into squares and sold at the ubiquitous *focaccerias* throughout the city. They are usually no thicker than 1 inch in height.

GRANDMA PIZZA A type of pan pizza, similar to Sicilian-style, in which the pizza is baked only once, with all its ingredients, as opposed to Sicilian-style, in which the crust is often par-baked and then topped and baked a second time. In some versions, thin slices of mozzarella cheese are laid over the dough before the sauce is applied to protect the dough. Umberto's and King Umberto's restaurants, both located in different parts of Queens, NYC, are credited with originally popularizing this style.

NATURAL FERMENTATION This is another term for sourdough leavening, as opposed to leavening dough with commercial yeast. See *Sourdough*.

OIL SLICK A technique I recommend for handling wet, sticky dough because wet dough won't stick to oiled hands or surfaces. It is useful for performing the stretch-and-fold steps, as well as for hand kneading on the work surface, by rubbing the surface with 1 to 3 teaspoons of oil to form a circular or rectangular slick.

PAN PIZZA I use the term in this book to refer to any style of pizza baked in a pan, whether round or rectangular, rather than directly on the hearth, such as is done with Neapolitan and NY-style pizzas. While not all pan pizzas utilize wet, sticky dough, as do the ones in this book, the pan does provide a solid frame that contains the dough and prevents it from overspreading.

PRE-FERMENT A leavened pre-dough, made with either commercial yeast or sourdough starter, that serves as a dough improver due to the flavor development accomplished during its fermentation. There are many varieties of pre-ferments (biga, poolish, pate fermenteé "old dough," as well as sourdough levain) but, other than the use of sourdough levain, the doughs in this book accomplish the fermentation flavor a different way, via cold, overnight fermentation, in which the dough becomes its own pre-ferment through long, slow development.

ROMAN-STYLE PIZZA This term has come to mean a style of focaccia-like pan pizza with inventive toppings, many applied after the pizza is baked. There are a number of variations or schools of thought regarding this style (Gabriele Bonci's Pizzarium versus Massimiliano Saieva's Roman Pizza Academy, for example), which include philosophical differences regarding dough hydration and flour types.

SCHIACCIATTA From an Italian word meaning "smash," this term relates to a type of Tuscan flatbread similar to focaccia. It is usually made in rounds but, like so many styles of flatbread, there are no real rules governing the shape. I consider it a Tuscan version of focaccia, though I'm sure many Tuscans would take umbrage.

SICILIAN-STYLE PIZZA
The Americanized version of a flatbread originally called *sfincione* in Sicily before migrating to New York, especially to Brooklyn, where it developed into a focaccia-like pizza embellished with lots of sauce and cheese. As it crossed the United States, many versions of this style evolved, but the most well-known versions are made in Brooklyn, NY at L&B Spumoni Gardens, where the crust is somewhat dense and creamy, and at J & V Pizzeria, with an airier, more open crust and where, the owners proudly told me, "We beat Spumoni Gardens in the latest popularity ratings."

SOURDOUGH A general term for naturally leavened dough and/or bread. While the term is mostly associated with San Francisco and, ultimately, the United States, naturally leavened breads exist everywhere, and they have been made for thousands of years. The sour flavor is primarily due to bacterial fermentation, and the leavening is caused by naturally occurring strains of wild yeast. Both the bacteria and the wild yeast are cultivated in a pre-fermented dough called by various names. See page 36 for more on sourdough.

SPIKING THE DOUGH A mixed leavening technique used by many bakers to take advantage of the flavor complexity provided by natural sourdough leaven, bolstered by the addition of a small amount of more concentrated commercial yeast. I suggest using this method for the sourdough crust recipe in this book to assure a rising time consistent with the doughs leavened only by commercial yeast.

STRETCH AND FOLD A method of strengthening the gluten network of dough by folding it by hand on an oiled work surface, followed by resting periods and subsequent cycles of folding. See page 22 for a photo depiction.

UNDERCRUST The bottom side of the pizza and, to many pizza lovers, the most valuable signifier of the quality of the slice. With pan pizzas, one of the goals is to achieve a crispy, buttery texture and taste, with a golden brown caramelization. This is achieved by a combination of high heat and a generously greased pan, either with olive oil or a combination of olive oil and melted butter.

WINDOWPANE TEST A way to determine if the gluten in a dough has developed enough to perform properly. See page 25 for a photo depiction.

YEAST, COMMERCIAL Properly known as *Saccharomyces cerevisiae*, it is a strain of yeast that can be reproduced easily in laboratories. It does not tolerate highly acidic environments but, because it comes to the baker in a highly concentrated form—either as a granular powder, such as instant yeast or active dry yeast, or in a moist block called fresh compressed yeast—it is able to ferment and raise dough in a very predictable manner. This is the same strain of yeast used to make many types of beers and wines (at one time, long ago, breweries would collect their leftover yeast and sell it to bakeries).

YEAST, WILD One of the two types of microorganisms essential for sourdough. While the strain is often identified in books as *Saccharomyces exiguous* (exiguous meaning "wild"), there are actually many strains of wild yeast that comprise a sourdough starter, too many to list individually, thus the generic exiguous. The important difference between wild and commercial yeast is that wild yeast is able to tolerate the acidic environment created by the bacterial fermentation, while commercial yeast cannot. See *Sourdough*, left, and also page 36.

ACKNOWLEDGMENTS

A book like this is always a team effort and, for the past 20 years, I've had the privilege of working with the always creative and collaborative team at Ten Speed Press. Thank you to everyone, including Aaron Wehner, Lorena Jones, Kelly Snowden, Kristin Casemore, and my editors Anne Goldberg and Ashley Pierce. Thanks also to the excellent work done by my copy editor, Brenda Goldberg, and proofreader, Ellen Cavalli. Thanks to the Ten Speed design team, led by Emma Campion, and designer Hope Meng.

This was my first chance to work with photographer Johnny Autry and his wife, food stylist par excellence, Charlotte. Collaborating with them and their team, Nick Iway, Mackenzie Tomrell, and Kali (Mustang) Miles Clark, was pure joy, as you can see from their amazing photos.

I also received great support from Evelyn Ainsley of LloydPans, who provided the beautiful deep-walled pans used in chapters one and three. Likewise, Paul Witke of Zimmerman Cheese, Inc. and Oscar Villarreal of BelGioioso Cheese, Inc. were extremely generous in supplying us with ample brick and Muenster cheese and various Italian-style cheeses. The spectacular salumi, nduja, and charcuterie were provided by La Quercia and Creminelli Fine Meats. Needless to say, we did some serious eating during the photo shoot.

Thanks also to my partners at *Pizza Quest*, Brad English and Jeff Michael, as well our directors and production team: David Wilson, Mark Dektor, and Annette Aryanpour. Frequent *Pizza Quest* contributors John Arena (pizzaiolo extraordinaire at Metro Pizza in Las Vegas) and Scott Wiener (founder of Scott's Pizza Tours, NYC) were also very helpful, especially for the Sicilian and Grandma section.

A special thanks to David Kazarian (owner) and Shane Lambert of Mash'd restaurant in Frisco, Texas, where Shane came up with the brilliant suggestion to embed half the cheese in the dough before the final rise (see page 15). That's how breakthroughs happen!

Finally, as always, the most important thanks of all goes to my wife, Susan, whose patience, suggestions, and eternal support made this all possible.

INDEX

A

Aioli, 174
Al Forno, 55
Amatriciana, Spicy, 146–47
anchovies
    adding, to pizza, 67
    Puttanesca, 153–54
Antico Forno Campo de' Fiori, 159
Arthur Bryant's Barbecue, 88
Artichoke Medley, Olive
        and, 97–98
arugula
    Bacon and Egg, 73–74
    Grape Tomato and Ricotta
        Cream, 161–62
    "Greek," 155–56
Avocado "Scampi," 173–74

B

bacon
    Bacon and Egg, 73–74
    Bacon and Potato Focaccia,
        132–33
    Motor City Hawaiian, 115–16
    Spicy Amatriciana, 146–47
    White Clams Casino, 151–52
baker's math, 20, 23
Banh Mi, 91–93
basil
    Pesto Genovese, 51–52
    Sun-Dried Tomato Pesto, 53
beef
    Beef Brisket with Burnt Ends,
        88–89
    Homemade Meatballs, 111
    Philly Cheesesteak, 112–13
    Reuben, 105–7
    Roast Brisket, 89
    Spaghetti and Meatballs, 109–11
Bianca, 159–60
Bianco, Chris, 2

Blue Cheese, Balsamic Onion
        Marmalade, and Walnut
        Focaccia, 127–28
Bonci, Gabrielle, 158
broccoli
    Lemon, Broccoli, and Garlic,
        100–101
    Veggie "Pepperoni," 95–96
Broccoli Rabe, Philly-Style Roast
        Pork with, 81–84
Brother Juniper's Cafe, 81, 105
Brown Dog, 2
Buddy's, 2, 66

C

cabbage
    Peter's Coleslaw, 107
    Pickled Vegetables, 93
Caffe Sport, 51, 173
Campanella's, 155
Canadian bacon
    Motor City Hawaiian, 115–16
Cauliflower, Kundalini, 78–79
cheese
    amount of, 12, 15
    Blue Cheese, Balsamic Onion
        Marmalade, and Walnut
        Focaccia, 127–28
    cubed, 11
    Grape Tomato and Ricotta
        Cream, 161–62
    half, on the dough before final
        rise, 15
    Lemon, Spinach, and Cheese
        Curd, 149–50
    Philly Cheesesteak, 112–13
    Ricotta Cream, 162
    sources for, 175–76
    types of, 9, 11
Chicago-style deep-dish
        pizzas, 65

chicken
    Banh Mi, 91–93
    The SCLT (Smoked Chicken,
        Lettuce, and Tomatoes),
        102–3
Citrus Glaze, 135
Clams Casino, White, 151–52
classes, 177
coleslaw
    Peter's Coleslaw, 107
    Reuben, 105–7
corned beef
    Reuben, 105–7

D

Detroit-style deep-pan pizzas
    about, 1, 65–67
    Bacon and Egg, 73–74
    Banh Mi, 91–93
    Beef Brisket with Burnt Ends,
        88–89
    The Classic Red Stripe, 69–70
    Garlic Lovers' Italian Sausage,
        117–18
    Kundalini Cauliflower, 78–79
    Lemon, Broccoli, and Garlic,
        100–101
    Motor City Hawaiian, 115–16
    Mushrooms to the Max, 85–86
    Olive and Artichoke Medley,
        97–98
    Pepperoni Deluxe, 75–76
    Philly Cheesesteak, 112–13
    Philly-Style Roast Pork with
        Broccoli Rabe, 81–84
    pizzerias known for, 177
    Reuben, 105–7
    The SCLT (Smoked Chicken,
        Lettuce, and Tomatoes),
        102–3

Spaghetti and Meatballs, 109–11
Veggie "Pepperoni," 95–96
dough
    adding flour or water to, 5
    amount of, 12, 15
    coarse, shaggy, 28
    dimpling, 11, 12
    gluten development and, 23–24
    Naturally Leavened Dough,
        33–35
    oil slick trick for, 31
    portioning and panning, 11–12
    stretch-and-fold technique
        for, 23
    time for making, 24
    White Flour Dough, 27–28
    Whole Grain Country-Style
        Dough, 29–31

E
Egg, Bacon and, 73–74
English, Brad, 95, 167
equipment, 5–6, 176

F
flour
    adding, to dough, 5
    high-gluten, 20
    measuring, 5
    sources of, 176
    types of, 8, 24
    See also dough
focaccia
    about, 1, 122, 123
    Bacon and Potato Focaccia,
        132–33
    Blue Cheese, Balsamic Onion
        Marmalade, and Walnut
        Focaccia, 127–28
    Focaccia Bianca with Herb
        Oil, 125–26
    Focaccia Rosso, 126
    Fruited Focaccia with Citrus
        Glaze, 134–35
    Herbed Tomato and Pesto
        Focaccia, 130–31
Frank Pepe Pizzeria
    Napoletana, 151
frico, 65
fruits
    Fruited Focaccia with Citrus
        Glaze, 134–35
    See also individual fruits

G
garlic
    Caramelized Garlic Cloves, 58
    Garlic Lovers' Italian Sausage,
        117–18
    Garlic Oil, 58
    Lemon, Broccoli, and Garlic,
        100–101
    Lemon-Garlic Sauce, 101
    Susan's Rosemary-Garlic
        Potatoes, 165–66
gluten development, test for,
    23–24
Grandma pizzas
    about, 139, 143
    Umberto's-Style Grandma
        Pie, 143–44
Grape and Anise Schiacciata,
    137–38
Grape Tomato and Ricotta
    Cream, 161–62
"Greek," 155–56
guanciale
    Spicy Amatriciana, 146–47
Guerra, Gus, 1

H
ham
    Motor City Hawaiian, 115–16
Herb Oil, 54

J
Jet's, 66
Jossi, John, 9

K
kale
    Grape Tomato and Ricotta
        Cream, 161–62
    "Greek," 155–56
    Susan's Rosemary-Garlic
        Potatoes, 165–66
Kundalini Cauliflower, 78–79

L
Lambert, Shane, 15
La Tona, Tony, 51
leavening, 8–9
lemons
    Citrus Glaze, 135
    Lemon, Broccoli, and Garlic,
        100–101
    Lemon-Garlic Sauce, 101
    Lemon, Spinach, and Cheese
        Curd, 149–50
Le's Sandwiches Café, 91
lettuce
    The SCLT (Smoked Chicken,
        Lettuce, and Tomatoes),
        102–3
Liguria Bakery, 2

M
Mama's Pizzeria, 112
Marinara Pizza Sauce, All-
    Purpose, 49
Mash'd, 15
measuring, 5, 8
meatballs
    Homemade Meatballs, 111
    Spaghetti and Meatballs,
        109–11
Mortadella, Sweet Onion-
    Béchamel with, 170–71

Motor City Hawaiian, 115–16
Mushrooms to the Max, 85–86
mussels
    Nduja Cioppino, 167–68

N
Naturally Leavened Dough, 33–35
Nduja Cioppino, 167–68

O
oils
    Garlic Oil, 58
    Herb Oil, 54
    Spicy Oil, 55
oil slick trick, 31
olives
    "Greek," 155–56
    Olive and Artichoke Medley,
        97–98
    Puttanesca, 153–54
onions
    Beef Brisket with Burnt Ends,
        88–89
    Blue Cheese, Balsamic Onion
        Marmalade, and Walnut
        Focaccia, 127–28
    Caramelized Balsamic Onion
        Marmalade, 56
    Motor City Hawaiian, 115–16
    Philly Cheesesteak, 112–13
    Philly-Style Roast Pork with
        Broccoli Rabe, 81–84
    Sweet Onion-Béchamel with
        Mortadella, 170–71
oranges
    Citrus Glaze, 135

P
pancetta
    Spicy Amatriciana, 146–47
Panopoulos, Sam, 115

pans
    greasing, 15
    materials for, 16
    shapes of, 16
    sizes of, 15
    sources for, 176
Parsley Pesto, 53
pasta
    Spaghetti and Meatballs, 109–11
pastrami
    Reuben, 105–7
pepperoni
    Classic Pepperoni, 142
    The Classic Red Stripe, 69–70
    Pepperoni Deluxe, 75–76
    Veggie "Pepperoni," 95–96
peppers
    Banh Mi, 91–93
    Nduja Cioppino, 167–68
    Olive and Artichoke Medley,
        97–98
    Pepperoni Deluxe, 75–76
    Philly-Style Roast Pork with
        Broccoli Rabe, 81–84
    Roasted Pepper Pesto, 53
    Secret Sauces, 59–60
    Sweet Onion-Béchamel with
        Mortadella, 170–71
pesto
    Herbed Tomato and Pesto
        Focaccia, 130–31
    Parsley Pesto, 53
    Pesto Genovese, 51–52
    Roasted Pepper Pesto, 53
    Spinach Pesto, 53
    Sun-Dried Tomato Pesto, 53
Peter's Coleslaw, 107
Philly Cheesesteak, 112–13
Philly-Style Roast Pork with
        Broccoli Rabe, 81–84
pineapple
    Motor City Hawaiian, 115–16
Pizza Quest, 2, 95, 167
Pizzarium, 2

pizzas
    baking tips for, 71
    creating new, 67
    great vs. good, 19
    importance of crust of, 19
    ingredient quality and, 6, 8
    types of, 1
    See also individual pizzas
        and styles
pizzerias, by style, 177. See also
        individual pizzerias
pork
    Banh Mi, 91–93
    Homemade Meatballs, 111
    Nduja Cioppino, 167–68
    Philly-Style Roast Pork with
        Broccoli Rabe, 81–84
    Roast Pork, 84
    Spaghetti and Meatballs, 109–11
    Spicy Amatriciana, 146–47
    See also bacon; ham; pancetta;
        prosciutto
potatoes
    Bacon and Potato Focaccia,
        132–33
    Susan's Rosemary-Garlic
        Potatoes, 165–66
Prince Umberto's, 143
prosciutto
    Susan's Rosemary-Garlic
        Potatoes, 165–66
Puttanesca, 153–54

R
Red Stripe, The Classic, 69–70
Reuben, 105–7
Reuben Sauce, 107
Ricotta Cream, 162
Roman-style pizzas
    about, 1, 122, 158
    Avocado "Scampi," 173–74
    Bianca, 159–60
    Grape Tomato and Ricotta
        Cream, 161–62

Nduja Cioppino, 167–68
pizzerias known for, 177
Rosso, 159–60
Susan's Rosemary-Garlic
Potatoes, 165–66
Sweet Onion-Béchamel with
Mortadella, 170–71
Root One Café, 78
Rosso, 159–60

S
Saieva, Massimiliano, 158
salami
Puttanesca, 153–54
Satellite Restaurant, 115
sauces
All-Purpose Marinara Pizza
Sauce, 49
Crushed Tomato Pizza
Sauce, 46
Lemon-Garlic Sauce, 101
making, 45
Reuben Sauce, 107
Secret Sauces, 59–60
store-bought, 45
See also pesto
Sausage, Garlic Lovers' Italian,
117–18
schiacciata
about, 1, 123
Grape and Anise Schiacciata,
137–38
The SCLT (Smoked Chicken,
Lettuce, and Tomatoes),
102–3
Secret Sauces, 59–60
shrimp
Nduja Cioppino, 167–68
Sicilian-style pizzas
about, 1, 122, 139–40
Classic Pepperoni, 142
"Greek," 155–56
Lemon, Spinach, and Cheese
Curd, 149–50

Puttanesca, 153–54
Spicy Amatriciana, 146–47
White Clams Casino, 151–52
sourdough starter, 36–38, 40–41
Spaghetti and Meatballs, 109–11
spinach
"Greek," 155–56
Lemon, Spinach, and Cheese
Curd, 149–50
Spinach Pesto, 53
square pizzas. See Detroit-style
deep-pan pizzas
stretch-and-fold technique, 23
Sun-Dried Tomato Pesto, 53
Susan's Rosemary-Garlic
Potatoes, 165–66

T
tomatoes
All-Purpose Marinara Pizza
Sauce, 49
Avocado "Scampi," 173–74
Bacon and Egg, 73–74
Banh Mi, 91–93
Beef Brisket with Burnt Ends,
88–89
Crushed Tomato Pizza
Sauce, 46
Grape Tomato and Ricotta
Cream, 161–62
"Greek," 155–56
Herbed Tomato and Pesto
Focaccia, 130–31
Kundalini Cauliflower, 78–79
Lemon, Broccoli, and Garlic,
100–101
Mushrooms to the Max, 85–86
Nduja Cioppino, 167–68
Olive and Artichoke Medley,
97–98
Philly-Style Roast Pork with
Broccoli Rabe, 81–84
Reuben, 105–7

The SCLT (Smoked Chicken,
Lettuce, and Tomatoes),
102–3
Sun-Dried Tomato Pesto, 53
Susan's Rosemary-Garlic
Potatoes, 165–66
Veggie "Pepperoni," 95–96
tools, 5–6, 176
Triple Beam, 2

U
Umberto's-Style Grandma
Pie, 143–44

V
vegetables
Banh Mi, 91–93
Pickled Vegetables, 93
Veggie "Pepperoni," 95–96
See also individual vegetables

W
walnuts
Blue Cheese, Balsamic Onion
Marmalade, and Walnut
Focaccia, 127–28
Pesto Genovese, 51–52
White Clams Casino, 151–52
White Flour Dough, 27–28
Whole Grain Country-Style
Dough, 29–31
windowpane test, 24

Y
yeast, 8–9, 36

Text copyright © 2019 by Peter Reinhart
Photographs copyright © 2019 by Johnny Autry

Published in the United States by Ten Speed Press,
an imprint of the Crown Publishing Group, a division
of Penguin Random House LLC, New York.
www.crownpublishing.com
www.tenspeed.com

Ten Speed Press and the Ten Speed Press colophon are
registered trademarks of Penguin Random House LLC.

Library of Congress Cataloging-in-Publication Data

Names: Reinhart, Peter, author.
Title: Perfect pan pizza : square pies to make at home,
    from Roman, Sicilian, and Detroit, to grandma pies
    and focaccia / Peter Reinhart.
Description: New York : Ten Speed Press, [2019] |
    Includes bibliographical references and index.
Identifiers: LCCN 2018054093
Subjects: LCSH: Pizza. | Cooking, Italian. |
    LCGFT: Cookbooks.
Classification: LCC TX770.P58 .R46 2019 |
    DDC 641.82/48—dc23
LC record available at https://lccn.loc.gov/2018054093

Hardcover ISBN: 978-0-399-58195-3
eBook ISBN: 978-0-399-58196-0

Printed in China

Design by Hope Meng
Cover design by Kara Plikaitis
Food and prop styling by Charlotte Autry

10 9 8 7 6 5 4 3 2 1

First Edition